DOO

Diane McCabe
6327 Sudbury Ct.
Oconomowoc, Wi. 53066
(414) 567-0135

A More Wonderful You

UNITY SCHOOL OF CHRISTIANITY

LEE'S SUMMIT, MO.

1959

A More Wonderful You

was first published in 1952.

This is the fourth printing.

This is one of a series of Unity books devoted to teaching how you can make your life better by applying Christian principles. The first Unity book, *Lessons in Truth,* was published in 1894 and is still in publication. The Unity work itself was established in 1889, when its founders, Charles and Myrtle Fillmore, began to share with others the Truth that had helped them.

The Unity movement now reaches millions of persons all over the world. Unity School of Christianity includes the Silent Unity department, to which thousands of people each year write for prayers for any need, and the Publishing Department, which distributes the Unity books and magazines that carry the Unity message around the world. Unity centers and churches are located in many large cities.

FOREWORD

This book is a compilation of articles that the readers of periodicals published by Unity School of Christianity have used and found especially helpful. The material was selected to provide a course in self-improvement for those who are trying to become happier, better, more successful people by putting the Jesus Christ teachings to work in their daily lives.

CONTENTS

Be Not Dismayed

THERE IS A solution for every problem. There is a cure for every ill. There is nothing in your life, absolutely nothing, that cannot be changed, corrected, and cured. There is no difficulty anywhere on earth that cannot be set right.

Truly this is a tremendous thought, but it is more than a thought. It is the Truth. If you know and accept the Truth, the Truth will make you free. You may not be able to understand or believe it now, but it is absolutely true that the present condition of your circumstances, your mind or body can be completely changed.

Your misery can become happiness. Your fear can become faith. Your confusion can become clear understanding. Your illness can become health. Your trouble can be taken away, dissolved. Though you cannot possibly see any way out, there is a way. Though you are certain your trouble is beyond any possible cure, there is a cure.

Whoever you are, wherever you are, whatever your difficulty may be, to you this is the word of truth: Be not dismayed; there is help for you. You may be plunged into the deepest despair. You may be engulfed in a depth of depression into which no flicker of light shines. You may be torn by the terror of one great fear or a multitude of fears. There are hope, and light, and assurance, and sweet

7

peace for you. There is an unfailing cure for you.

You have done something that you believe cannot be undone? Someone you love has hurt you seemingly beyond any possible mending? You have an illness of mind or body that has been pronounced incurable? Still the answer comes with all the force of Truth behind it: there is change, mending, cure complete and utter for you. Lift up your head; lift up your heart. There is a dawning light, there is a safe and sure retreat, there is a victory, there is happiness, and there is peace for you.

No empty, idle promise is this, no illusion, no mirage to lead you toward still deeper despair. It has the power and reality of the universe behind it. It rests on the one great law of life. It is the word of God.

You want to be free from the difficulties in which you find yourself? You have cried out in agony of spirit for relief, but the darkness does not lift, the sorrow does not go away? You cannot get away from it? Try this method then.

Start with the premise that you have been created by God, the Father Spirit of all life. Believe that God is infinitely good, that there is no wrong of any sort in Him. He created you, and gave you life from Himself. He made you in His own image. The life in you is God's life. Therefore it is good, just as He is good. The real you, the spirit that God created, is good and perfect. Try to believe that.

God took the real you, the spirit, and gave it a body and a mind. He left your mind free to direct it. Whether you realize it or not, it is your mind now that is causing you your trouble, and it is your mind reaching inward to the true you and bringing it out that can cure it.

No longer blame any other person or circumstance for your condition. No longer blame yourself. Have done with making your problem the center of your thinking. Think instead that actually God is the center of your life, the core, the primary reality. The circumstances that surround you, the thoughts that twist and tear you are not the true reality at all.

If you can get to the real you, which is God in you, and start expressing your true self in your thinking, you will slowly but surely see the change coming. Thought by thought, step by step, day by day you will see your mind changing. And miracle of miracles, as your mind changes, conditions change, other people change for you, your whole life changes. That is the amazing truth.

Cease to say to yourself: "I am unhappy. I am miserable. I am ill. I am in the grip of conditions and circumstances from which there is no release. I have been injured beyond healing. I am unable to rise above my fears and troubles."

Say rather: "I am made for happiness. I am made for health. The Spirit of God within me is perfect in every detail. I am that Spirit. I am the conqueror of all things through God who is in me. I am not weak. I am immeasurably strong. I am able through realization of the God power within me to rise above difficulties, whatever they are. I am able, and I will."

Do not dismiss this as something you cannot understand. Do not say it is foolish theorizing. Try it. Give it an honest trial. It will work. It is God's everlasting Truth.

—*William A. Clough.*

Passport to God

JOY! Joyous! Rejoice!

Are not those inspiring words, jewel-like in their sheer beauty? Spoken, they delight the tongue; written, they enchant the eye; heard, they are rarest music to the ear. And the reason is that for countless generations the human mind has identified these words with the lively emotion of happiness.

Like any other beautiful thing, a lovely word has great value. And the emotion for which the word joy stands is of the utmost importance in the daily life of every person. Joy is one of the major gifts God has bestowed upon man. In fact, it furnishes the speediest, most efficacious method of putting ourselves in tune with His Spirit.

That last may seem a pretty strong statement. But it won't if you will pause to recall how nearly impossible it was to contact God when fear and worry and anxiety had crowded all joy out of your mind. It is true that a swift call in the midst of sudden stress, such as an accident, may have forced its way through. But no matter how great any person's intellectual perception of God's instant availability may be, until that cold perception has been animated by the warm emotion of joy, contact with the source of all good will be spasmodic and confused and highly unsatisfactory.

11

You see, joy is a passport to God; and we always receive it when we truly appreciate that He is waiting, ready and willing to solve every problem that may confront us. In other words, our intellectual perception is brought to life by our emotion of joy so that, joined, they make the glorious recognition that lifts us right above our difficulties and troubles. It furnishes us the power to reach the high place within our own self, where God dwells, that blessed place where peace and health and happiness and poise and prosperity and success are everyday occurrences.

Have you ever noticed the different strata in the earth's surface? They can be seen on the bare rock face of a mountainside or in a dirt bluff where an excavation has been made. Distinct layers are visible, one above the other. And just as there are these different strata of rock and clay and earth, so are there different "layers" or levels in each person's consciousness.

It works like this. When a person is unhappy, fearful, depressed, disappointed, defeated, he has allowed himself to descend to a very low stratum of consciousness. And since like attracts like, he will soon find himself encountering people and experiences of a very disagreeable nature. Let him remain on this level of thinking, and before he knows it he will find himself overwhelmed with sickness, lack, and troubles of every sort. They will simply swarm in like the vermin they are; and he need not blame them for his discomfort because it is no one's fault but his own: he has crawled down into the mental sewers where vermin dwell.

What can be done when this happens? Well, sitting there wailing and crying out to God to come and help will not change the condition. God does not descend into the negative depths to rescue us. No, indeed! If we want to reach Him, we must bestir ourselves and fight up through those mental layers of negation until we win to where He and all the goodness and fineness and riches of life are to be found.

I know that sounds terribly hard. But truly it is not. For all we have to do to make the ascent is to lift our thinking and keep it lifted. Nothing can keep us down when we resolve to go up and stick to that resolve. Raise the consciousness! It will blaze a way through!

You see, God has made each of us a free soul. We have the privilege of dwelling in whatever mental stratum we desire. So that if we really want the good things of life, then what we need to do is to make our thinking reach the high level where God dwells. Believe me, there are beautiful, rich gifts from God eternally traveling toward us from every side; but the majority of us keep our consciousness at such a low level that the health and money and good job and happiness and love and friendship intended for us pass right over our heads.

A few years ago my world crashed about my
ears. I was left with an intellectual perception of
God and His availability; but I was so weighted
down with grief and loneliness and self-pity and
fear of the future that joy was a forgotten quantity
in my life. It is true that I repeated affirmations and
prayers; but without joy to animate them they were
mere lifeless mouthings. I studied, and read, and
thought that I was trying to reach God, but I
could not find Him. As I went on dwelling in the
low stratum where grief flourishes I began to experience financial lack, my health became poor, and
finally I lost interest in living.

I had always thought life a marvelous adven-
ture; so that to waken in the mornings with nothing
to look forward to was a horrible experience. I
think there can be no state of mind more frighten-
ing than the state of black depression that so poisons
us that our enthusiasm for life seems to die. Even
the color appeared to have left natural things like
flowers and trees and blue skies so that I saw everything in black and white and leaden gray.

I passionately love color, and when I lost appreciation of it I roused myself and began to fight
upward. I said to myself, "You have wallowed in
grief long enough! You have contemplated trouble
and sorrow until you have become their slave. Why
shouldn't your health leave you when you have consistently abused it? Why shouldn't you know lack
when you have spent your days learning to fear

lack? Why should you have friends when you are such a dismal companion?"

I accepted the full blame. But I also knew that if I could contact the living God I could recapture the good things that give life meaning. And right there true logic said to me: "If you want to find the path to the kingdom where God dwells, start thinking about Him. For as you turn toward Him He will turn toward you."

How to think about God, that was the question. Well, I began to enumerate His qualities. I thought of beauty and strength and courage, of peace and love and joy. In my unhappiness the most desirable seemed to be joy, and as I concentrated on the contemplation of this quality I started my climb upward.

The things that I did may sound ridiculous, but you can believe me when I say that they worked. First of all I threw open the windows and let in God's fresh air. I thanked Him that He had supplied it so abundantly and that I was alive to breathe it. Then I turned on the radio to the gayest dance tune I could find. My limited lesser self sneered cynically as I began to dance and sing to the music. It told me I was a fool and an idiot; but I laughed in its face and danced all the harder.

The result? It was not ten minutes before I felt like a new person! I ran to the mirror and was amazed to see how my eyes had lost their lackluster expression. I had color in my cheeks, the corners of my mouth were turning up instead of down, and suddenly I knew that life could be enchanting and marvelous fun again and that there were still thousands of new things for me to learn and do and be.

From that day I began to count my blessings, to be grateful and friendly and generous. I endeavored in every way I could to show my gratitude by helping others to find the way out of their difficulties. And certainly the things I did were efficacious; for by raising my consciousness to the level where God reigned I began to experience what seemed like miracles. Within a year I had my own lovely home, the garden I had dreamed about, exactly the car I wanted, a greatly enlarged income, a delightful circle of new friends, and the wonderful peace that passes all understanding.

The Psalms are wonderful helpers when joy eludes us. Some of them are true elevators to carry us to our true dwelling place, which is the kingdom of heaven. Over and over the Psalmist seeks to arouse our emotion of joy. Note how he urges us: "Sing!" "Praise!" "Lift up!" "Give thanks!" "Trust!" "Bless!" "Hope!" "Love!" "Make a joyful noise!" Remember how he says:
"Oh let the nations be glad and sing for joy;
 For thou wilt judge the peoples with equity,
 And govern the nations upon earth.
 Let the peoples praise thee, O God;
 Let all the peoples praise thee.

The earth hath yielded its increase:
God, even our own God, will bless us."

The lotus is called the sacred flower of India. It begins its climb upward from the very depths of noisome bogs, even deeper than where serpents dwell. Up through filth and slime and stagnant waters it pushes its joyous, confident way until one day it rises out of the depths into God's sunlight where it bursts forth in a display of entrancing beauty.

If your climb toward the light seems arduous, remember the lesson of the lotus. Remember also that where God is good is. Summon joy and let it lift your thoughts and words and emotions to the impregnable height where you may dwell safely forever under God's protection, providence, and loving care.

FOR MEDITATION

I rejoice in the goodness of God, and my affairs overflow with good.

—*Belle Burns Gromer.*

It's the Give in It

"How far do you think a set of those heavy steel tires would run on paving before wearing out?" I asked a blacksmith who was putting a new set on a heavy log wagon.

"Oh, about three thousand miles," he answered. "These are the best made, but it wouldn't be more than that."

"What would be the top milage on those tires?" I asked an automobile mechanic who was putting a new set of rubber balloons on a car.

"Hard to say what the top would be," he replied. "Some run as much as forty or fifty thousand miles. These should give at least thirty thousand, I should say."

"Do you mean to say that a rubber tire will run on paving ten times as far as a steel one before wearing out?" I demanded.

"That's right," he answered. "You see, it's the give in it."

A great light began to dawn on me. Strange as it may seem, in some situations rubber outwears steel, and does so because it is more pliable. It adapts itself to the irregular surface of the road, and thus reduces wear and tear to the minimum. The rigid steel wagon tire never shapes itself to anything, but crushes and grinds its way along. It takes the full shock of each bump and is ultimately worn out by its own hardness. Rubber runs longer because it has give in it.

This is not a freak of nature, but conforms to a law of life. It may seem a paradox, but it is true. Hardness of spirit, attitude, viewpoint, may seem a protection, but it is likely to prove just the opposite. It takes relaxed pliability to survive the bumps. The person who solves the problem most quickly and easily is not likely to be the one who gets tough but the one who adapts himself to situations. Pliability outlasts hardness. It has give.

The philosophy back of national aggressions is not supported by the results. The governments that were built upon it bear tragic witness that the more brittle anything is the more likely it is to break.

At the same time individuals and peoples who live by a philosophy of sweet reasonableness seem to endure and get on. They have their stretches of rough road to travel, of course; but their adaptability enables them—like the rubber tire—to take the bumps undamaged. This seems to be the way in which gradually and ultimately the meek inherit the earth.

In a certain picture drama a great sorrow suddenly threatens a young wife. As she seems about to surrender and be crushed by it her husband suggests that if she will make friends with the trouble it will lose its power to overwhelm her. She tries the formula and finds that it works. It was the give in it.

That is the way with adaptable people who meet things in relaxation of spirit. They are like rubber tires, passing easily, smoothly, and safely over roughnesses that would scrape, scratch, grind, and damage rigid steel. The softer material has found the way to make peace with its problems. It has give in it.

Two people meet the same kind of trying experience. One grows angry and resentful, because he has a rigid soul. The other takes it with a patient smile. Two people have the same kind of difficult task to perform or problem to meet. One approaches it with rough hands and clenched teeth. The other approaches it as he might a pleasant diversion. Two people have closed doors to open. One pounds away with a battering ram. The other gets a key. There is no question as to which will outwear and outperform the other.

This is not a suggestion to temporize with anything that is wrong or untrue, but rather that the standards of right and truth can be lifted higher by gentle hands. A rubber tire does not destroy its nature by declining to be cut to pieces by stones in the road. It remains just as much a rubber tire as it was before. It has merely demonstrated its ability to take what for the moment cannot be helped. Not only is it true that what can't be cured must be endured, but it is also true that there is a way to endure it without damage to oneself. The secret is the give in it.

Rigid souls have rigid viewpoints, and rigid minds devise rigid sets of rules. The old saying that light moves only in straight lines was long considered axiomatic, and it was said that human action should therefore do the same, regardless of anything whatever.

But it was never true that light moves only in straight lines. When light strikes an object, large or small, that part of it which is not absorbed by the object simply slips around the barrier and proceeds on its way. We have dawn and twilight because the rays of the sun bend their course around the earth, announcing the coming of the sun before it rises and reminding us of its passing a while after it has set.

The newer voices in science are now saying that light never was bound strictly to straight lines but that its action, like many other things in nature, is relative. Tomorrow we may be saying that the operation of everything in the universe is relative to the operation of every other thing. The Creator has given us a universe of co-operative and interacting parts. In other words, God has made things so they have give in them.

One can be ever so true to his ideals and purposes and yet refuse to let his soul be scarred and bruised by the things that go contrary to them. To yield to temporary defeat only unfits one to win the final victory. Patience and the ability to take things as they come are not mere conformity;

they are common sense. Rubber-tired heroism wins more triumphs than the rock-ribbed, iron-bound variety. The law of averages makes it so, for it lasts longer and has more opportunities. The same is true of the person with the milder voice and the gentler hand.

One of the surest ways to waste one's time and strength is to spend them settling scores. The steel-tired soul looks for opportunities to ride down and crush those it feels have trespassed against it, only to find that revenge is not sweet, for there is no human revenge. The avenger always finds himself ultimately face to face with the Lord's dictum: "Vengeance *is* mine; I will repay."

The rubber-tired spirit knows a better way, the way of forgiveness. It has learned from the Master that people who trespass against one do so because they do not understand, and that they are to be pitied and forgiven rather than hated and punished. When man forgives he rises to a level very near the divine. He always wins a true and lasting victory, whereas the avenger never wins any victory at all. It's the give that makes the difference in the results.

The people who complain most about adversity may be the people who have the least adversity to complain about. The trouble is not that they have so many troubles but that they have not learned how to meet the experiences of life. They do not yield to the rough places. They have not learned how to take the bumps on the road. They should contemplate and try to learn wisdom from some of those who have met the storms of life over a long road and yet press on with a smile of confidence and courage.

The ambitious young man who plans to reach one of life's towering pinnacles should consider carefully how he proposes to go about it. To storm the gates of success with a steel-wheeled chariot is just the way not to do it. There is an approach at which they will open. The wise man learns this secret first. Few of life's true rewards can be taken by force, and none of them can be kept by it. The road to the heights is rugged: it will wear out the heavy shoes of grim determination, even as it will speed the feet shod with confidence and faith. It's the give that does it.

FOR MEDITATION

I make peace with my problems. I know that God is adjusting all things, and I am relaxed and adaptable to His will.

—Clarence Edwin Flynn.

Self-Confidence

PICKING UP an old issue of a well-known periodical the other day, I read from an article this statement: "Confidence in self attracts the confidence of others."

I pondered a bit over the assertion. Confidence in self—self-confidence: how often these expressions are misused and misunderstood! How often they are mistakenly used, or interpreted to mean confidence in the personal or objective self, the physical or mental self.

What is real self-confidence, self-confidence that is worth while; that will not only get you where you want to go but will sustain you there when you arrive; that will really draw to you the confidence of other people? Is it confidence in the outer self, the self that *seems* to be you or I; in the mortal, fallible self whose judgment is too often founded on the appearance of things, on the symbol rather than on the Truth back of the symbol?

No! True self-confidence is confidence in the inner self—the self that is our part of God; therefore the right kind of self-confidence is in reality confidence in God. It is confidence that there is always a Power behind us that will not let us fall, that will guide us unerringly if we comply with the divine law; confidence that, through you and me, divine law will express just what we want and will *sustain* us in that expression. Too often people seem to attain great things through false self-confidence, only to lose those things in the end, or to gain little or nothing spiritually through possessing them. A man may, it is true, amass a fortune, or achieve fame in a career, merely by exerting mental power. But how often, upon the failure of that power, when he is personally unable longer to sustain it, does his fortune vanish, his fame crumble, leaving him worse off than before, because he has lost faith in himself.

There is a confidence in the personal, the mortal self, that will often seem to accomplish much. It will sometimes pull us through a crisis if our strength does not fail; it will sometimes put us on a high pedestal for a time. But the kind of self-confidence that relies wholly upon Spirit within us is sure, serene, established, unwavering, perfect in operation and permanent in results. Knowing that there is always that within us which knows, when we have learned utterly to trust to its guidance and to follow it in all things, we shall not fear the final outcome of any situation, or fear losing what we have gained; and we shall be free from the sense of strain imposed by the self-confidence that relies only on personal powers. The latter kind of self-confidence is but a crutch for a lame man; the former is permanent healing for his lameness.

"Let go, and let God." This is the basis of real self-confidence, the kind of self-confidence that realizes that we can do nothing of ourselves, but that, if we are willing to comply with law, the Father within us does His works. A young man was limited to a wheel chair. For a long time he had tried to demonstrate healing through faith, but finally he became desperate. It is often said that man's extremity is God's opportunity.

One day this man was holding in his hand a little motto that read, "Let God!" He sat in mournful meditation. He was getting nowhere. Why?

The motto slipped unheeded to the floor. In an agony of supplication, he implored God for light —to know what he had *failed* to do in his efforts to comply with divine law. (He had sense enough to know that not the law, but he, had failed.)

Glancing down—not by chance, for nothing ever transpires by chance—his eyes fell upon the little card lying at his feet. In some way the last letter had been hidden, and the motto now read, "Let Go."

There was his answer! He had been trying too hard—trying to do the thing himself, when there was a higher power ready to do it for him. He had been using the wrong kind of self-confidence.

Discarding confidence in the mortal, fallible, changeable self, he became imbued with confidence in the immortal, infallible, immutable self—the inner self that is, always has been, and always will be one with God. And he gained his heart's desire, as all of us will gain our desires the moment we can assume that attitude.

There is always that within us which knows, which is pushing forth into expression as fast as we will let it. The moment the petty personal self gives way, opens the channels, washes the clay from its eyes, the whole being is flooded with light, illumination, understanding; the real self begins to do its work, and we find that we are at last on the right path. The only way to remain on the path is to follow our divine Way-shower by knowing always that "the Father abiding in me doeth his works."

This does not mean that we are to "slump" in our efforts to do well that which it is given us to do, because we have decided to leave the manner and the method to divine guidance. "Whatever thy hand findeth to do, do *it* with thy might." Spirit expresses through you and me. You may be the power behind your saw, but you want the saw itself to be sharp, shining, and properly set.

You are the tool which Spirit must handle, the chisel with which it may at this moment be endeavoring to carve out some wonderful, useful, or beautiful creation; so keep yourself sharp, shining, and ready. Say to the inner mind, with all your heart, "Here I am—use me."

Continually asking Spirit within us what to do, and how to do it, watching carefully for Spirit's leading and following it whenever we discern it, is the earnest practice of the presence which will finally establish us in the right kind of self-confidence—the self-confidence that makes for joy, constructiveness, and permanence in all our work.

Such self-confidence *must* draw to us the confidence of others. Why? Emerson says, "In all conversation between two persons tacit reference is made, as to a third party, to a common nature. That third party or common nature is not social; it is impersonal; is God." There is, then, something in others that answers to something in us, and that something is Spirit—because we are all one in Spirit, whether or not we have yet reached the period of development in which we have a conscious recognition of this truth. We are not always one in outer personality—and that is where an antagonistic spirit often arises.

When a man has great faith in God and in the divine working out of affairs, he instinctively trusts God and turns to Him; but the hard, blatant, sure-of-himself, know-it-all type arouses in thinking people little but opposition and enmity—or pity. Such persons realize instinctively that his is the wrong kind of self-confidence; that he is building not on a sure foundation, but upon the sand, and the first wave of misfortune may wash away his fine edifice.

On the contrary, when a man has confidence in the great law's working out his affairs for him and confidence in himself as working with this law, then he has found the real and most effective form of self-confidence, the self-confidence that will inevitably cause the people whom he needs in his life to gravitate toward him. He is going to achieve, and achieve greatly.

FOR MEDITATION

God has not given me a spirit of fear, but of love and power and of a sound mind.
                              —*Wright Field.*

Chronicle of Blessings

MY FRIEND had many troubles. As we walked home together in the young spring night she confided one of them to me. "And the worst of it is," she concluded, "that I'm powerless to do anything about it!"

"Not powerless," I said gently. "You can bless it."

"Bless it!" she exclaimed, looking at me sharply to see whether I was joking. Noting the seriousness of my expression, she went on: "Well, I may as well admit that I'm desperate. If blessing will do any good, I'm willing to try it. But you'll have to explain what you mean."

I explained. As we stood under the white and purple lilacs at her gate, I told her why I believed in the power of blessing to change things in one's life, and I related a number of instances where blessing a problem had worked seeming miracles. She listened intently, the lines of worry in her face gradually softening. What I told her was this:

At first the suggestion that we "bless" something seems rather whimsical, rather like carrying a rabbit's foot or hunting for a four-leaf clover. The skeptical person will probably leave it at that. But the man who wants to see for himself will inquire more deeply. When he does he will find that the power of blessing derives from the same source as the power of gravitation and is every bit as much a law. That is, it works not on chance but on principle, one of the foremost principles of life itself: unity.

Truth students know the importance of right thinking, that as a man thinks within himself, so he is. Right thinking becomes easier when we know that basically all things are good; that there is something in every person, thing, and condition that is blessed and worthy of a blessing.

Most of the great religions of the world teach unity; that is, that God is the creator and source and that all things are a manifestation of Him in varying degree. Most of us are willing to accept this teaching. It is emotionally appealing and intellectually reasonable. Where we fail is not in our disbelieving it but in our forgetting to practice it. In our hours of meditation it may seem clear to us that God is all, in all, and over all. But when problems beset us and things go wrong, when our world is suddenly thrown out of gear, then we are prone to look at the surface of things. God does not enter into our plans, or He enters only as a very uncertain quantity. Then we "judge . . . according to appearance." The divine side, the hidden soul of things, is then, for us, as nothing.

When we bless a problem, an injury, a lack, or a foe, we acknowledge the divinity in the situation or the person. We as good as say, "I behold the good (God) in this also!"

Paul counsels, "Bless, and curse not." One of the definitions of the verb "bless" is "to consecrate or hallow by religious rite or word; make or pronounce holy."

The word "holy" stems from the same root as the word "whole" and in itself denotes unity. That which is whole is undivided, complete, perfect. To bless is to "make or pronounce holy" the person, thing, or event that troubles us or about which we are concerned, declaring it to be one with us in divine harmony or wholeness.

Those who know me find it difficult to believe that I was once a chronic worrier. I would worry for days at a time. The frightful situations and disastrous events I could conjure up in the course of a few minutes of worrying would have done credit to any nightmare. Of course I knew theoretically that worrying is a waste of time. I had been able to observe conditions long enough to know that most of the things I worried about seldom came to pass. But I worried nonetheless.

When the first Truth literature came into my hands it struck root almost immediately. I saw that here was a philosophy both dynamic and reasonable; and what was even more important, it was practical. I set to work at once to prove its lessons for myself. Despite my efforts at overcoming, one fault remained adamant: I still worried. Though I tried sincerely, I seemed unable to overcome the habit. Then when I needed it most I came upon this paragraph in Lowell Fillmore's book *New Ways to Solve Old Problems:*

"The power of blessing is amazing. You can cultivate the power of blessing by beginning now to bless everything that comes into your life. Bless your home. If you have old and worn-out rugs, clothes, and furniture, bless them, and you will see something happen that will surprise and please you. Things and persons that you felt like condemning will begin changing and will begin bringing good to you. The power of blessing will actually build a new world about you."

Begin now to bless everything that comes into your life.

I took these words as my slogan; and though at first it was difficult for me to see any improvement either in myself or in my surroundings, I persisted. At that time my personal finances were one of my greatest problems. Almost three quarters of my husband's salary went to meet obligations before living expenses could be met. I literally could see no way out.

But knowing better than to dwell on the why and how of it, I consistently blessed our money. I also blessed the empty shelves and worn clothing, the sparsely furnished upstairs rooms, the bedding that in cold weather had to be augmented with coats.

Gradually things began to change. For one thing I seemed suddenly able to "smell" a bargain the way a good reporter "smells" news. I always seemed to be on hand when there was a good value to be had or some "unadvertised special" was available. I suddenly became inspired with countless ideas for making over and making do. My friends complimented me on my ingenuity, though I previously had shown little talent or inclination in this direction. Friends gave me things—"just what I wanted!" —time and time again. An old bedspread was given me, for instance, worn in the middle but with enough good material left out of which to contrive drapes for a small room. Scores of instances like this proved to me beyond a doubt that there is a power in blessing greater than we have as yet realized and that it is infinite because it stems from God.

I could go on for many more pages, furnishing a whole sheaf of testimonials out of my own experience alone. Rather I would suggest that you prove this law for yourself.

Bless your money. See it for what it truly is: a symbol of divine substance poured forth without limit to meet all your needs over and above demand.

Bless your debts in the certainty that it is the Father's good pleasure to provide you with enough to discharge every obligation of yours.

Bless your body, and see it manifests radiant wholeness. The Spirit is life, and the Spirit dwells in you. Know that nothing can withstand its healing presence. Unify yourself with divine perfection by blessing every organ and function of your body. Bless away troublesome physical conditions. Recognize perfection, and by the sure working of divine law perfection will reveal itself through you.

Bless your problems. Even if you feel, as my friend did, that you are powerless before the tide of events, a blessing will call forth good where you can now see only evil. A woman whose husband was told by his doctor to move to the West Coast if he wished to retain his health, consistently blessed the move, though to all appearances it meant ruin for them both. Neither one was young. It was during the depression years, when work was hard to find. Yet out of that move came a life of greater happiness and fulfillment than the two had ever known. Where they had lived before they had known only the limiting surroundings of an industrial area. The work that the man did was monotonous and demanding. Now they have a small poultry ranch and orchard, involving work that both of them love and that neither one considered as a possibility. Best of all, they have the satisfaction of having taken God at His word and "proved" Him.

Bless your food as you prepare it for the table. Bless your mail, and it will reach its destination safely, bringing joy and good to the recipient. Bless your work, and you will find new inspiration and efficiency in performing even the most difficult task.

Wherever there is a lack slip in a blessing. You can bless an empty purse into plump abundance, empty shelves into blessed sufficiency, an empty heart or an empty life into the fullness of joy.

I do not ask you to take my word for it. I am only one of many who by practical application have proved the law. It is up to you to prove it for yourself.

FOR MEDITATION

I improve the things and conditions in my life by blessing them.

—*R. H. Grenville.*

About Eating

GOD gives us as much of His vital spiritual substance with our food as we are willing to accept. If we accept the food we are eating at its physical value and think of it only as composed of material elements, we are appropriating only a part of the substance that God is attempting to give us. His food is designed to feed the whole man: spirit, soul, and body. When we eat merely to satisfy our bodily hunger we cannot absorb into our being the full value of the nourishment that God has prepared for us.

In recent years science has discovered that in addition to the well-known fats, proteins, sugars, starches, and minerals that compose our food, there are certain other substances that are very necessary to the proper nourishment of the body. These they have named vitamins.

Vitamins are recognized chiefly by their effects upon the body. Insufficient quantities of vitamins cause physical disorders in the body. Lack of vitamin B causes lack of appetite, lack of vitamin G causes retarded growth, and so forth. Science has named the vitamins, but this naming does not mean that it has completely solved the mystery of their nature. These names probably are not the names by which God calls them, and they doubtless would be as potent by any other names.

There are other facts about food that are not yet understood. There are spiritual elements in connection with food that can be recognized and appropriated only by those who eat their food with spiritual understanding.

We all realize that different bodies react toward food in different ways. Certain foods that are good for most people may be poison to a few. Some persons are allergic to certain kinds of food and they do not know why. One may be allergic to the food that is most healthful and palatable to others. The mental attitude has much more to do with the effect of food upon the body than the average person realizes.

Back of all food is God's perfect idea of substance. If we desire to get the best possible results from our food we must realize this truth and consciously and thankfully accept this mystical idea of substance. If we fix our attention upon God's substance as we eat we shall set free potential qualities in our food that are even more helpful than vitamins.

Seldom does anybody ever obtain all the possible benefits from the food he eats. For just one week try eating your food slowly, blessing each mouthful as you dedicate it to God's service and glory. You will note that your food will taste better and that it will digest more easily than before. Even the spinach, parsnips, or carrots that you did not particularly care for before will have a new and pleasant flavor.

If you will eat one kind of food at a time this experiment will be easier. Food eaten in this way will increase your vitality and you will require less food to satisfy your hunger. You will not feel logy or sleepy after such a meal. Your mind will be clearer and more alert, because you will use less energy to digest your meal. It requires a larger amount of energy to digest an oversupply of food.

Never indulge in worry, hate, fear, or sorrow while you are eating. If you are disturbed, sit quiet a few minutes before you begin to eat. Affirm the presence of God several times before you begin the meal. Realize that you are surrounded and filled with His presence. Make room in your mind for praise, good will, happiness, love, and rejoicing. Eat slowly to the glory of God as you rejoice and you will build health into your body. You will thus be able to co-operate with God more efficiently in His plan to keep your body well and whole. You will eat to satisfy the finer needs of your body, not to stuff it.

There is a healing intelligence in you that is always trying to keep your body in repair. Every cut and bruise is looked after by this intelligence, and if you co-operate with it by supplying the right food vitalized by your blessing, it will do a more nearly perfect job for you.

Try for one week "eating" God's word as you eat your meal. Do this joyously and note the results. This will not mean that you need become a bore to your family and friends. If you do not care to explain to them what you are doing, be pleasant company while you dedicate your food to God. Do not enter into negative conversation but if possible try to turn it into something constructive, sweet, and happy.

Do not be worried if you fail sometimes to bless every mouthful. It is not so easy to do. Be patient and keep on trying. I believe one week's trial will be so helpful that you will want to continue eating to the glory of God always.

FOR MEDITATION

Father, I thank You for this daily bread and also for the spiritual bread of life that is Your loving gift to me.

—*Lowell Fillmore.*

Faith When It Is Needed

I ONCE KNEW a man who had a habit of praying, using just two words. As he went about the business of living his life, from the moment he woke in the morning till the moment he fell asleep at night, every time he felt a need, which was often, as it is with all of us, he would say, "Now, Lord!" He would say it aloud, or under his breath, or silently in his heart, and face his problem, or his duty, or his desire with that one affirmation. I could see that his prayers were answered in terms of his heart's desires.

I never heard him explain his habit, but nobody who knew him long could fail to know what his habit was, or to see his good results. It was not hard to understand his thinking; he carried all his heart's desires in his heart, and he knew that God knew his heart. He did not think it necessary to tell God every time and all the time what his heart's desires were, and to enumerate and define them all anew when any one of them came uppermost. "Now, Lord!" was to him like a push button that he could touch at need, and turn on the light and the wonder-working power of God in his affairs.

In Hannah Whitall Smith's book "The Christian's Secret of a Happy Life" she tells of a woman who was a constant inspiration to everyone with whom she came in contact, and who helped innu-

41

merable people to find faith, who used continually a
four-word statement whenever she faced a problem,
her own or another's. Whenever a doubt or a fear
or a puzzling situation came up to be dealt with,
she would say to friend, stranger, or self. "But there
is God." The statement evidently gave her peace;
and peace gives people ideas, or gives ideas a chance
to get to them; and ideas are the means by which
they solve their problems.

Of course anyone who has such a habit of dealing
with his own or the problems of others is sure to
have made some provision for emergency by pre-
paredness. It cannot be otherwise. We might say he
has a spiritual bank account on which he can draw
checks at a moment's notice—checks that do not
"bounce." He lives by Jesus' mandate, "Have faith
in God," and in moments of stress he cannot be surprised into panic; he is "quick on the draw," as our
westerners used to say—but in the sense of drawing
checks, not guns.

Our impulses in time of emergency, which we
call instinctive, are always in keeping with our habits
of thought. In a sense we act without thought, that
is, we act without conscious reasoning when the demand for action allows us no time to consider logical-
ly the pros and cons of the situation. But we never
act without being impelled to do so by what we
have stored up somewhere in our inner self, in our
subconsciousness, which has established conclusions
that determine our action.

Much as our bodily glands respond to sudden demand, what we might call our "spiritual glands" act instantly when we are faced with a spiritual demand. In our body our salivary glands release their juices the moment we merely think of food; our suprarenal glands pour adrenaline—which in a sense might be called liquid courage—into our bloodstream, the instant a strong emotion, such as fear, is excited in us. Just so our spiritual "glands," which generate the "juices" of love, kindness, honesty, magnanimity, can and will open instantly to send their flow into our life-stream.

In his little booklet *The Golden Key,* Emmet Fox says that any trouble will vanish if we turn from it to a thought of God. He recommends that we use the four-word affirmation, *"God is with me,"* as a means of reminding ourselves, of bringing what we have habitually thought about God to bear upon all problems of any kind. Indeed, as one friend of mine suggests, we need only one word for such a reminder, if our habit of mind is to think about infinite love and omnipresent power as real and available to us. The one word God contains, and will always contain for us, all we know about Him, all that our faith includes concerning His relationship to us.

Did it ever occur to you that most of our English words that most nearly include the attributes of the Deity are short words, such as love, truth, life. "God" is the shortest. I once asked a Spanish gentleman what was his word for Christ. "Él," he said, which translated into English means "He." There is only one "He" for the Spanish man of faith.

Now what all of us want is instantaneous access to our greatest resource in time of stress, isn't it—whether the stress is danger or delight? Does it seem odd to call delight a stress? Literally happiness can be overwhelming; in sudden prosperity we need strength and wisdom quite as much as in sudden adversity. In fact, prosperity may be "harder to take" that adversity. We need help to handle our blessings, too. It is always at hand if we have the *habit* of faith in God.

The point here is that what we need when we cry for help is God. If we want God to be with us in emergency we have to "keep Him around" at all other times as well. We have to make a companion of God.

Brother Lawrence, a monk, made a life business of seeking the awareness of God, that he might be conscious of God's presence with him *all* the time. We have to practice the Presence if we are to have it, whether as a source of help in time of trouble, or as a source of peace when peace is needed. So it is our daily, hourly, momently thinking that counts for us when we are suddenly "under fire."

We sometimes meet ridicule when we talk about right thinking in the presence of people who think we mean a dream-come-true kind of wishful thinking. Only our habit of thinking in positive terms

will save us from feeling humiliated by such ridicule.
But nobody can hurt or shame us by making fun of
us when we have the kind of faith that comes of
living in God's presence. So too, at times when un-
expected praise or applause comes our way because
somebody admires our attitude and its results, we
may find it spiritually dangerous to accept this praise
to ourselves if we have a habit of taking credit to
ourselves for the good that comes to us. If habitually
we credit God with our blessings, we shall be in no
such danger.

The closer our sense of companionship with
God, the less likely we are to suffer from ridicule
or applause, from danger or safety, from fear or
rashness, from timidity or conceit, from confusion
or monotony, from prosperity or adversity, from
anything at all. "Thou wilt keep *him* in perfect
peace, *whose* mind *is* stayed *on thee.*" "If ye abide
in me, and my words abide in you, ask whatsoever
ye will, and it shall be done unto you." I should like
to italicize the words *keep, perfect, abide, whatsoever,* and *done,* to emphasize them, but whether we
do or do not emphasize the words, these lines cover
the matter. If our mind is stayed by habitual thinking of God, if we abide in Him, we shall never be
upset or lose out.

But more than this, habitual thinking of God is
sure to put us into such a healthy, receptive condition that blessings are automatic. Our reactions to
stress will be like those of structural steel in building,

or bridge, or ship, to the forces of shifting winds: adequate to the emergency.

But all the similes and metaphors there are cannot express the wonder of experience to the man or woman or child whose constant habit is faith. It is often said that we cannot force faith, or even find it, all at once when disaster or loss threatens. True, too, when sudden riches or "luck" or cheers from the grandstand menace our stability. But we can build faith, cultivate it, absorb it, ingrain it in our heart. We can think unceasingly in terms of faith, act upon it constantly, make it steadfast.

All affirmations of Truth are good, all turning to God is right. But the best time to affirm is when the stresses are low. The time to cultivate your garden best is not when storm and flood are at their highest. The plants that root deep and grow woody stems are not mushrooms, but sturdy perennials that are planted or set out in quiet weather.

I find a kind of planting that helps is a careful, painstaking seeding with the idea that whatever happens, God is using me. If you and I cultivate this consciousness till it becomes conviction, we can induce the growth of faith in ourselves stout enough to meet anything. If God is using me, nothing else can matter, can it? I have no occasion to worry, I can relax, no matter how the wind blows, or the guns roar. "There shall no evil befall thee."

Nothing that seems to be evil shall prove to be anything but good, if God is using me. No charge or

fear that I am a shallow fool or silly optimist can
upset or unsettle me. For God uses our weakness,
our folly, even our wrath, as well as our better qualities, to praise Him—if we keep turning our all
over to Him.

So in times of emotional upheaval we need not
feel that it is imperative that we repeat the 91st
Psalm, or the 23d, or the 62d, or the Sermon on the
Mount, or any other Scripture, if it is our habit to
think in their terms in time of relaxation. Indeed, if
our relaxation times are filled with faith thinking,
we shall find that the peace we experience in relaxation is seldom disturbed in us in times of stress,
that it extends to cover greater areas of our life than
we might suppose possible. Peace will become a
woody-stemmed habit that will endure storms and
floods too. The peace that "passeth all understanding," will pass the stresses also.

"God is using me." I need not even think of
myself as a tool in His hand, which He is bound to
keep well ground and oiled and free from rust; I
am a part of Him, and my life is His. My fitness to
be used is like the fitness of a hand to a healthy man.
I need not doubt my skill; He develops the skill in
me that He wants to use.

God may want to use me merely as a weight
in His scales rather than as the cutting edge of a
tool; what does it matter to me, so long as He makes
use of me? He may want to use me as a messenger
rather than as an executive; or as a reflector rather

than as a light; as a listener rather than a voice; as a spoke rather than a hub in one of His wheels. But He will use me for all I am worth, and I shall be worth far more in His use than I could possibly be otherwise. What matters is my consciousness of being used and useful, in the right place at the right time for the right purpose, which gives me a sense of rightness in my life.

"God is using me." That is a seed which, if planted in our heart and cultivated awhile, will grow and bear extraordinary fruit—faith when it is needed.

FOR MEDITATION

Now, Lord, I claim my good.

—*Gardner Hunting.*

God-Given Talents

WE OFTEN hear a person say: "Oh, I don't have any talent. I can't sing or write or play a musical instrument. I'm just an ordinary person with no special ability." Invariably he adds, "But I wish I did have a talent."

Are you one of the persons who says this? Well, you have scores of talents, God-given talents, ready to be used to bring more good things into your life, and to make other lives happy too.

First of all let us find what the word talent means. Webster defines it as "the abilities, powers, and gifts bestowed upon a man; natural endowments;—thought of as a divine trust." We know God has bestowed gifts upon each of us. But do we think of them as talents, as abilities, powers, and gifts, as a divine trust? Do we use them as we would use one special talent to add to the well-being of ourselves and others? No, we take them for granted; consequently we do not appreciate or use them to the fullest extent, with the result that we lose much of the joy of living that could be ours.

What are the God-given talents that we all possess? There are so many we cannot enumerate them all, but here are a few.

Our first great talent is the ability to think. Truth students know that positive, constructive thoughts outpicture themselves in a well-balanced, happy life.

But do we always think constructively? No, we allow negative thoughts to creep into our consciousness, and unless we immediately check them we jeopardize our life. We have the power, and certainly we should consider it a divine trust, to control our thoughts. We know right thinking is the basis of every kind of good, so why not help your good come into manifestation by using your talent to think right? Remember "as he thinketh within himself, so is he." I have found it helpful to take as my motto "No thought offensive to God shall enter my heart or mind."

We have the talent to believe. Jesus did not speak idle words when He said, "All things whatsoever ye pray and ask for, believe that ye receive them, and ye shall have them." Sometimes we do not understand the full significance of the word believe. We hear it often and use it glibly without remembering that it means "to have faith or confidence . . . to exercise belief or faith." Notice the active verbs "to have" and "to exercise"; they do not imply a passive wishing or hopeful day-dreaming but a strong, virile faith that recognizes God in every situation. When we truly believe, we have a sense of sureness, a feeling of security, a serenity, a quickening of the inner man to an awareness of the presence of God. When we have the consciousness of such oneness with the Father, we truly believe and can rest assured that the promise "I have meat to eat that ye know not of" has real meaning for us.

We have the talent to bless. By blessing each seeming obstacle in our pathway, we bless it right out of existence. I am reminded of a woman who was greatly troubled because, as she said, a certain person kept "messing up" her life. She wanted to know what to do to eliminate this person's interference, which she declared was making her unhappy. I told her every time she thought of the person to say "God bless you," instead of allowing thoughts of dislike or resentment to enter her mind.

She was skeptical at first that this would help her but decided to give the "blessing idea" a trial. She called me some time later and joyfully exclaimed: "I don't know what happened, but that person isn't bothering me any more. I feel a great release, and I don't even have any more dislike or resentment toward her in my heart." If any person, situation, or condition is bothering you, instead of fussing about it try the blessing method and sincerely mean the blessing. Don't rattle off a few "God bless you's" and expect a miracle to happen. The blessing must be sincere; it has to come from your heart, and you have to be linked in consciousness to God within you.

Certainly Jesus knew what He was talking about when He said, "Bless them that curse you." In other words, bless anything in your life that seemingly harms you and you remove it. Be generous in your blessing, and remember that each blessing you send forth sincerely and prayerfully returns to you in "good measure, pressed down, running over." Could you ask for anything more?

We have the talent to praise, which many of us unwittingly overlook or forget. We take for granted everyday things people do for us, with never a gesture of thanks to them. We should remember that people thrive on praise and usually do their utmost to deserve more, providing it is wholesome praise and not flattery.

Praise is another way of expressing appreciation. Nonappreciation promotes headaches, heartaches, and estrangements, while real appreciation establishes harmonious relations. The next time some person hurts you or the children do something that irks you try the praise method and watch the happy results.

Close to the talent of praise is the talent of thanksgiving. Here again we take too much for granted. Let each of us for one week be a thanksgiver, full of thanks for all God's gifts, whether extended to us through the hand of a fellow man—which is also God's hand—or through nature as it unfolds before our heretofore unseeing eyes. "With thanksgiving let your requests be made known unto God" are words of truth.

The best way to increase anything is to give thanks for what you already have; use that as a basis for the increase you desire. Remember that Jesus Himself thanked the Father before the thing He desired came into manifestation. Just as Jesus did you must raise your consciousness to where you recognize the presence of God in and around you. It is the recognition of the power, the spirit, behind the words that gives the increase. When you feel gladness welling up within you at the recognition of the divine within you, then and then only do you say, "Thank You, Father," because you know that "all things whatsoever the Father hath are mine." The outward manifestation follows this inner recognition.

We have the talent to sing. Maybe you will never be an opera or radio star, but you can "sing unto Jehovah a new song," a song of hope, of thanksgiving, of faith, of love, of courage, of praise, of joy, of blessing. The best tonic in the world for an aching body or heart is a song.

A young man was so badly burned in an explosion that the doctors gave him up to die. He said afterward, "I knew what the doctors thought, but I also knew that if I could sing I'd get better." So he sang and sang and sang. He recovered, and he is probably still singing! How about you? Do you "sing praises to Jehovah" when things look dark? "A cheerful heart is a good medicine."

We have the talent to forgive. If you say, "I can forgive, but I can't forget," then you are forgiving with your mind only, not your heart. Unless you can forgive and also forget you are not truly forgiving. By forgiving we help ourselves more than we help the other person, because when we remove the resentiment from our heart, we give God a chance to come in and manifest Himself. Please notice that Jesus put it this way: "Forgive us our debts, as we also have forgiven our debtors." In other words, we must forgive freely if we expect to be freely forgiven. We must also ask God for forgiveness for our own mistakes and shortcomings. The time to forgive others is when we feel free from our own trespasses, when the slate is clean.

To pray is one of our greatest talents. The perfect prayer is the Lord's Prayer, as taught by Jesus, which contains all things necessary for man's well-being both spiritual and material. It gives the key to getting along with people; it unlocks the treasures of the kingdom when we are ready to receive them. Prayer is talking to God not only as a friend but as our Father, to whom we may confide our innermost secrets. But heed Jesus' words "When thou prayest, enter into thine inner chamber, and having shut thy door, pray to thy Father who is in secret." In other words, your prayer is something between you and God; it is not to be broadcast to other people, so put silence upon your lips after praying. To pray without ceasing does not mean to spend all your time in meditation and prayer but rather to make your life a prayer, your daily living a constant and conscious recognition of God within you at all times.

We have the talent to work. Occasionally when my work seems monotonous or tiresome I recall these words of Henry van Dyke:

"Let me but find it in my heart to say,
  When vagrant wishes beckon me astray,
'This is my work; my blessing, not my doom;
  Of all who live, I am the one by whom
This work can best be done in the right way.' "

After repeating these inspiring words I am renewed and strengthened. Surely my work is my
blessing, because I know I am the one who can best
direct the lives of my three children into Godlike
paths. Not only that, but Jesus said, "The works
that I do in my Father's name, these bear witness of
me." I try to do all my work in my Father's name.

The list of our talents is endless. We have the
talent to radiate joy, to serve, to heal, to learn, to
play, to laugh, to grow, to love. These are all
constructive talents. They could all come under one
heading—the talent to love, for when we love we
perform all these talents naturally. God is love,
and we are a part of God. Therefore we are also
love, God in manifestation.

Now we come to the most important talent of
all, the talent to do. We may know something of
Truth, we may talk about Truth, we may think we
are in Truth, but unless we do something about it,
it is as nought. Did not Jesus say, "If ye know these
things, blessed are ye if ye do them"? No matter
how much Truth you know, how many books you
have read, the intellectual grasp you may have, unless you use it, it does not do you or anyone else
any good. If in your life you want more spiritual

growth and unfoldment, which in turn brings you happiness and all the things that make for more abundant living, use the talents that have been bestowed upon you as a divine trust.

A man who asked Henry Ford for work started to explain that he had been in a penitentiary. Mr. Ford interrupted him to say: "I don't care about your past mistakes. Start where you stand!" Start where you stand to use your God-given talents. "Now is the acceptable time," and that means now.

Your God-given talents are a glorious gift to you personally from your own indwelling Father. He asks nothing in return. Yet one of these days when you are so happy, so free, so joyous, so prosperous, so peaceful that you exclaim to yourself, "Why didn't I do this before!" you will hear Him whisper, "Well done, good and faithful servant: thou hast been faithful over a few things, I will set thee over many things; enter thou into the joy of thy Lord." You will know what He means, because you will already have entered into the joy of your Lord.

FOR MEDITATION

I put my Good-given talents to use, and God adds to and multiplies my abilities.

—Christine Mabry.

Imagination

LIFE IS NOT always a matter of physical inheritance. In its inception it has its source in God the primal energy that inheres in all things. One of our greatest means of contacting life, energy, and power is our imagination.

Webster says that imagination is the act or power of forming mental images of objects or things not present to the senses, hence mental pictures of new ideas. In other words we form pictures in our mind's eye.

Imagination is a medium through which we make conscious connection with Divine Mind. We use it constantly, consciously or unconsciously, so it behooves us to learn to use it aright and thus identify ourselves with our true being.

All mankind has the power of imagination, of making mental pictures, of seeing things with the mind's eye. It is one of God's choicest gifts, for it is one He used to produce the universe. "God created . . . in the image of God," that is, according to the "imagination" or idea or picture that He held in mind.

The first command of God was "Let there be light." Light we recognize as understanding, thought, ideas. The great tragedy is that so often our ideas are dark instead of light. They are negative instead of positive. We get our feet wet on a rainy day and at once we have an idea, a picture of a cold. We plan a vacation, think of taking a journey, and we at once begin to wonder if we have sufficient funds, thus creating a picture of lack. We wonder if the train or bus or plane will be wrecked, if our automobile tires will hold out. We have an idea, a picture, of disaster. We form mental pictures of what we do not want and then wonder why bad luck, as we call it, dogs our footsteps.

The things we continually picture in our mind are what will be outpictured in our life. This is the law. There is an old saying that seeing is believing, but we in Truth should turn it about. Instead of saying that seeing is believing we should say believing is seeing! If we believe a thing is possible of accomplishment we can see it with our inner eye and work toward it, and soon we can see it with the outer or physical eye, soon it will become manifest for us.

What is our greatest desire right now? Is it health? More money? A different environment? Health for a loved one? Friends? A job? Success in some undertaking?

First ask yourself whether this is right with Christ. Will He approve of this? If you can truthfully answer yes, relax, close your eyes, let all tenseness ease out of taut nerves, tired muscles, bound organs. Turn your mind inward, where it contacts the mind of God and mentally see yourself in possession of that which you desire.

See yourself surrounded by friends if that is

what you want. See yourself in your desired environment. See yourself doing the work you want to do. Behold yourself possessed of health, radiant, vitalizing, rejuvenating health. See yourself as you would be if you possessed abundance.

Open your mind, assume a receptive attitude, and let your desire flow forth to you.

Do not doubt.

Do not question.

Do not begin to wonder how your desire may take form. Simply see yourself as you desire to be.

While you are in this receptive mood quietly give thanks to God for the abundant good He is showering upon you. Do not tell God how you want it to come. Just thank Him that it is come.

When you have finished your silent contemplation do not return to a state of negative thinking. Do not drop your picture of fulfilled desire. Bless and give thanks continually. Keep your imagination working. Refuse to see anything but what you want. See yourself always as strong and vital and happy, free to do the work you love, surrounded by kindred souls with whom you can share the fruits of your victory.

Use your imagination to create the pattern of what you desire to see manifest in your life. Use your power of thought to draw from infinite Mind all the ideas relating to the particular goal toward which you are striving. When you have the picture perfected, when you can see yourself doing what you want to do, then start doing something about it. Do the first thing that comes to mind. God speaks to us through ideas. Be alert to catch these ideas.

If your desire is to paint, get the materials together and start painting. If it is to write, start writing. Use the same tactics you would if you wanted to bake a cake or build a house. You would first assemble your ingredients, your materials, and then you would begin to work with them. You would do something about your desire, knowing full well that it would take more than wishful thinking, more than dreaming, to produce the thing you want in usable form.

That was the method Jesus Christ used, as you will see if you read the Gospel account of healings He performed. He pictured perfection in His mind; then called it forth by some action on the part of those He healed. Read His commandments. To the man with the withered hand He said, "Stretch forth thy hand." To Lazarus He cried, "Come forth." To the man born blind He said, "Go, wash in the pool."

So it is with us, when we see perfection in and about us we call it forth by applying ourselves to whatever Spirit leads us to undertake. With the dawning in us of the Holy Spirit we feel equal to the solving of all our problems and in this state of mind we are confident and courageous.

Imagination is power. What you picture—image —in your mind day after day and week after week must come to pass. "As he thinketh within himself, so is he." We think in pictures. What we picture we produce.

If we keep seeing ourselves as sick, we shall never be well. If we keep seeing ourselves as poor and downtrodden and out of our desired environment, we shall never rise above lack and inharmony, we shall never succeed; for "as a man thinketh within himself [seeth in his mind], so is he."

A thought held steadily in the mind will grow and increase until it fills the entire consciousness. That applies to a positive thought of Truth or a negative untruth; so it is most important that we keep to positive thinking.

If you seem to have problems to meet today in the home, in your business, or in your work, just get quiet a moment and acknowledge—see—the Christ presence straightening out all your affairs. See divine order established. Picture to yourself the Christ righting your problem. A new idea, an apt word, a feeling of security will become yours so that you can begin at once to work out your problem according to the Christ standard.

In Truth we always remember that we are channels through which good flows, we see things as they are in their Christ perfection, and we declare, "The Father abiding in me doeth his works." We take the picture and God develops it into reality!

Consecrate your power of imagination, of vision, to God today. God through you sees all things as they are in Truth. Your way is now made clear. It lies before you as a bright, beautiful avenue of opportunity for joyous service and true attainment. Your mind is illumined and inspired as you follow His guidance.

Writing to the Corinthians, Paul said: "The natural man receiveth not the things of the Spirit of God: for they are foolishness unto him; and he cannot know them, because they are spiritually judged." True judging requires that we use our mind's eye to see the reality or the good that underlies any adverse or negative situation.

To human sense it may seem foolish to say that we are well when to all outward appearances we are sick; to say we have plenty when our purse is empty. Yet in Spirit there is only health, there is only plenty. Our business is to turn our vision toward health and plenty and hold it steadily there as we go our human way. We hold our thoughts steady to Truth, our eyes on our goal until that which we see with our mind's eye is made manifest to our visible sight.

"The light of the eyes rejoiceth the heart."

"Lift up your eyes on high, and see who hath created these."

FOR MEDITATION

The light of God illumines my life, and I see my affairs in perfect, harmonious adjustment.

—L. Stevens Hatfield.

The Unfolding Truth

WE TOOK some guests from inland for a drive along the coast one day. It was a particularly scenic ride through historic old towns, along wooded roads, and past beautiful seashore views.

We thought, "How interesting this is, how beautiful! It is good to be traveling here." All our thoughts were positive. We were happy.

But after a while we became aware of increasing heat and heavier traffic. We began to talk about it. Then we were tied up in a long line of cars, halted because a drawbridge had jammed. It was growing late. We were many miles from home. Our thoughts were negative; we were unhappy.

Actually we were delayed less than an hour, but in that time our mental attitude was so altered that we scarcely noticed the scenery on the drive home. It was as beautiful as it had been in the morning, but our eyes had become clouded by negative thoughts.

How unfortunate, I thought, that the bridge had to get stuck and spoil our day. Then the voice of Truth whispered: "It isn't the bridge. It's you. You spoiled your day. You entertained the wrong thoughts. You wasted a golden hour in fretting when you might have been talking to God."

We took the drive to provide enjoyment for

our guests, and ourselves. The object was good, and
as long as we kept our attention fixed on good the
experience was good. When we turned our attention
to the unpleasant the experience was unpleasant.

Truth reveals to me that this principle applies
to every phase of life. The object of life for all
of us is to provide happiness for others and for
ourselves. God has provided fully for its attainment.
But we cannot realize it unless we keep our attention
fixed on it.

We are all much alike. Our problems are basically the same, though they may take different forms.
The cause and the cure are always the same. Just
as our inability to enjoy the beautiful scenery after
the bridge episode was due to our getting away
from God, so every seeming difficulty of whatever
nature confronting us is caused by our separation
from Him. The solution of every problem and the
cure for every ill is to return to the presence of God
and consciously abide there. We can do this by
prayerfully controlling the direction of our thoughts.

In one of his books Emmet Fox prescribed a
seven-day "mental diet" that he guaranteed will
change for all eternity the life of anyone who scru-
pulously follows it. The diet is simply to refrain
from entertaining a single negative, destructive
thought for seven days.

Anyone who has tried it knows it is not easy.
It means entertaining only positive and constructive
thoughts every minute of the day. It means abiding

consistently in the presence of God, never wandering.

Since I have been attempting to practice Truth principles as taught by Unity School, I am amazed at the amount of negative thinking I have been doing all my life. I am amazed at the tenacious hold that thought habits have on me. But I am most amazed at the transforming power of the positive thought.

Let me give some examples. I may get up in the morning feeling God's presence and enjoying a sense of well-being. Then I look out of the window and discover it is beginning to rain, and the first negative thought comes: "Rain will upset all my plans." I stoop to put on my shoes and a pain shoots through my back. The second negative thought comes: "Perhaps I am getting arthritis."

So it goes, and within an hour the trend of my thinking has slipped to the negative side of things, and I am beset by a multitude of seeming problems. The hundred and one occurrences of the day as well as thoughts of past happenings and of future possibilities assail my mind, agitating and disturbing me.

Does not something like this happen to most of us in a greater or less degree every day? It does not happen to the person who persistently and consistently practices the revelations of unfolding Truth. His mind is orderly, his thoughts are positive.

I see that I must change my thinking, and when I do, the consequences change accordingly. I look out at the rain and think: "That is good. It is good for the grass and the crops. It does not matter about my plans. I will make other plans. God is not changed, nor is the good He has prepared for me changed."

I turn my thought from the appearance of pain or illness and think of my body as whole and perfect, as it is in the sight of God. I keep my thought on the perfection and not on the seeming imperfection and move toward the realization of the perfection and away from the appearance of imperfection.

All the way down the line I refuse to think negative, unhelpful thoughts. I refuse to criticize or condemn. I refuse to recognize and give place to evil, since I know that it is not real. I do not shut my eyes to reality; I open them to reality!

Mortal eyes see heartbreaking conditions in the world today just as they saw them when Rome ruled the temporal world. Jesus saw the conditions too, but His heart did not break, for He saw through and beyond to the reality, the Truth. He saw all men as children of God, endowed with the Father's divine nature. He saw their infinite possibilities. Through the appearance of evil, through the torture and the seeming defeat of the cross He steadfastly kept His attention fixed on God, seeing beyond the appearance of utter disaster to the truth of complete victory.

Jesus Christ summons us to be His followers, His brothers in the Father's universal family. He calls us to overcome all fear of every sort and to see with the eyes of faith straight through to the Father's unfailing love and care.

I do not grasp it all at once. My faith is not yet full enough to help me heal myself instantly of infirmities or to banish all negative thinking. Still I cry, "Lord, I believe; help thou mine unbelief."

But as my understanding of Truth unfolds under the wise and gentle guidance of Spirit I find faith developing within me. A new understanding of an idea comes. I see with a new clarity what Jesus meant by some phrase or parable that He spoke.

When I am absolutely true, when I do the very best I know, when I am receptive and responsive to the highest degree of which I am capable at the moment, I feel a steadily growing sense of well-being. The faith principle works.

Take some little examples. I cannot by force of will stifle a tickling in my throat that causes coughing, but by concentrating on God and denying any power to the irritation I find that it goes away. I cannot put myself to sleep by counting sheep or by other mental exercise, but I find I can go to sleep almost at once by turning my full attention on God and away from troubled thoughts.

I have found that what seems to be a serious problem is solved pleasantly and satisfactorily when I trust in God and refuse to be anxious about the outcome. I have found that all financial needs are met when I work diligently and refuse to worry about how they will be met.

Trusting in God, I feel safe and secure. I feel assurance that my loved ones are likewise safe and secure wherever they may be.

The Spirit of God in me is all good. Everything I think or do that is not good separates me from Him and from a full realization of my good. Everything I think or do that is good unites me with Him.

So when a negative or critical thought comes into my mind I refuse to hold it. When a physical ailment appears I correct its cause by denying its power and affirming God's power.

The Truth is forever unfolding new vistas, taking on added meaning as my perception grows. It is the unchanging, eternal Truth, but every day I see new ways of applying it as I am carried forward toward the goal of perpetual dwelling in the presence of God.

I cannot recapture the lost hour. But I have this hour and all the hours ahead. My Father is with me, and I do not want to waste a single minute of any hour. To relax and grow in His presence I must constantly keep my thoughts on the positive path. The unfolding Truth teaches me the way.

FOR MEDITATION

I know that only the good is worthy of my attention. I love the good. I center my mind on the good. I enjoy the good.

—*William A. Clough.*

Say It for Goodness' Sake

ONLY THE FOOD that you take into your mouth becomes a part of you. The food that you leave on the table can have no part in your body. So it is with words. Those you take into your mouth become a part of you and those you do not repeat have no part in you.

In order to speak ill of anyone we must take ill words into our mouth, and when we do they become a part of us. Often we think we are meting out justice to offenders when we criticize them, but by taking these words of hate and shame into our mouth we are incorporating them into our mind and then they disturb our poise and happiness. Such words take our attention away from constructive methods that, if followed, might prove to be helpful to erring people. We must remember that when we say nasty words they are in our own mouth and they can do little there to reform the culprit.

There may be times when we should speak out and deny evil, but usually to do so is simply to eat poisonous words and hurt ourselves without helping to solve the problem. We increase the confusion of the world by adding our voice to the already tempestuous sea of negative voices. It is not helpful to our cause nor does it improve world conditions to join in faultfinding or "kicking" or in cursing some public official who has been made

the target of public ill will. When we do these
things we eat a heavy meal of inharmonious words
which sinks us into the realm of inharmony.

After we indulge in a spree of criticism and
gloomy talk the sky seems to become overcast and
the joy of life goes under a temporary cloud. We
can by foolish words sell ourselves on the idea that
world conditions are very bad and that God has
apparently forgotten us. Neither do we improve the
morale of people we have thus condemned.

Our desire should be to help people out of
their difficulties, and we cannot do this by heaping
a confusion of negative words upon them. We must
learn how to lift them up instead of depressing
them. Jesus came to save sinners, not the righteous.
Why not follow His example?

Every outer condition has its inception in the
mind, and it must be corrected in the mind before
it can be permanently healed in the outer world.
Harsh words and blows do not cure misunderstand-
ings nor can they make angels out of devils. Every
change for the better must be made first in the
heart and mind. Good words touch the heart more
effectively than critical or hurtful words. Confusion
in the outer world stems from confusion in the
mental world. Because harmony must be established
first in the mental realm, contentious and bitter
words can in no way restore harmony.

Remember that good words taken into our mouth
bring happiness and prosperity into our life, while

destructive and unkind words confuse us. Angry
words interfere with the digestive processes in our
stomach and upset other functions of our body.
When you give someone a good tongue-lashing you
harm yourself more than you do your target.

The world today needs good, encouraging words
more than anything else. Who will speak these words
of Truth? No one can do it better than you and
I. We have a wonderful opportunity today to do our
bit in establishing peace on earth and good will to
men by using words of love, good will, and forgiveness. Why add to the world confusion by grip-
ping when we can join in the heavenly song of praise
to God for peace on earth, good will among men?

There is need today for men and women who
have sufficient faith in the goodness of God to stand
still and see His salvation and then declare it to
all men. Those who do this will not go unrewarded,
for in blessing they will be blessed.

Man cannot live on material food alone, but
if he would truly live he must eat the words that
proceed out of the mouth of God. Thus did Jesus
answer Satan who tempted Him to turn the stones
of the wilderness into bread in order to satisfy His
hunger.

We are today faced by the same temptation.
We are trying to subsist on the hard conditions of
material world experiences represented by the
stones. There is no nourishment in words of criticism concerning evil. To resist evil is indeed one of

the temptations of Satan. Our soul will starve on such a diet. Our truly nourishing food comes from the words of God, which are words of Truth and righteousness. God's creations are all good, and when we speak His good words we eat the bread of life. Why feed upon the stones of life when we can have the real bread?

You cannot grow and prosper on a diet of stones. Neither can you grow and prosper on hard words. The love, life, and Truth of God are the true bread of life. These are embodied in Christ, the Son of God, who is with you always. Listen to Christ and be nourished and live. He will feed you as Jesus fed the five thousand in the wilderness. Take only His good words into your mouth. Let your conversation be composed of words that are filled with the constructive vitamins of Spirit. Let your words serve the purpose of building up and distributing the peace of God.

So when you have anything to say, say it for goodness' sake.

FOR MEDITATION

"Let the words of my mouth and the meditation of
*   my heart*
* Be acceptable in thy sight,*
* O Jehovah, my rock, and my redeemer."*

                                            —*Lowell Fillmore.*

The Adventure of Years

"MY COUSIN John was very sick. The doctor said so, and John agreed. When I went to visit him he was in no mind to receive any cheerful word. He talked of his various misfortunes at length. He recalled some members of the family whom we had both loved. The 'old folks,' he called them. Then he said: 'They are all gone. My God! we are the old folks now!'

"I couldn't stop John from being 'old folks,' but I vigorously denied that I belonged in that class. I had my job and the health and energy to do it. Beyond that I had faith in God as a Father. I believed in the forward-going impulse of life, and I lived accordingly.

"That was fifteen years ago. John did not get well. He departed from this life, which had become to him a vale of tears. I'm still taking care of my job. Today it takes more time and effort and carries more responsibility, but my health and energy are still sufficient. I have not become 'old folks.'"

When Mary told this incident, we who knew her agreed that she had not become "old folks." She was expressing the eternal youth of the spirit that goes on in confidence to the place where the way turns sharply upward.

What shall we do about the race thought that says old age and failing powers must come after certain years? It presses upon us from all sides. The doctor says, "You must take it easy. You're not as young as you used to be." Our friends say, "We're not getting any younger." The family says you must not take those long walks at your age or do some of the other things that we are accustomed to doing. If we agree with these verdicts we are done with active life. We might as well retire and nurse our woes. But if we dissent we must do something intelligent about it.

For dissent does not mean conflict. We do not tell the doctor he is talking nonsense. We silently deny his statement of limitation while we heed all the good advice he is giving us. When the old friend, excusing some dereliction of his own, murmurs, "We're not getting any younger," we smile and say, "Oh, but let us stay as young as we are." When the family urges the cutting off of some activities, we know that their love for us has lapsed into anxiety. We say nothing about it, but we go on doing the things the inner Spirit bids us do.

For individually we must do something to dislodge the mischievous race thought of old age and failure. We are not going to move the whole race at once. All growth is slow. The leaven that "leaveneth the whole lump" is just a bit of yeast when it is put in the large measure of flour. What you and I say today may seem to count nothing against the great mass of false thought, and indeed it may seem to do very little for us ourselves. But it is the bit of leaven. It needs time and warmth to grow into power.

There is evidence that large groups of people are beginning to lay hold on the truth that old age and failing powers are the creation of our own mind. The peasant woman of prewar Europe accepted old age at thirty; she felt, acted, and looked old. She should have been just entering the period of the maturing of the mind and greater productivity.

When I was a child my grandparents were old people. Looking back now, I realize that they must have been in their early fifties. They spoke of themselves as old; they looked and acted old. Now fifty often opens a decade of accelerated power and accomplishment. It ought to. At fifty one is just beginning to gather the wisdom of experience and put it in the form of a working philosophy.

"Retire at sixty?" asks the wise man of affairs. No! He is well and strong. And the eternal Spirit within him, never young, never old, is in command. If he should consider the counsels of the material world he might begin to consider retirement. But if he listens to the truth of the inner voice he knows his life assurance is in going forward.

A few days ago in a public dining room a woman stopped at our table to speak to us.

"What a charming woman," said one of the group.

"Yes," said another, "charming, and more. She is a living challenge to all of us. She had her eighty-

seventh birthday last month, and she is still going
on with the work to which she has devoted herself
for the past twenty years."

There was in that group at the table a woman
of fifty who had just been talking about her limitations and deprivations. She had listed in too much
detail her lack of health and had finished with that
blighting phrase "I suppose I must expect such
things at my age." We hoped that she might get
some of the meaning of the life of the eighty-seven-
year old woman who would never cease going forward. But we all had to notice that she looked older
than the woman of eighty-seven.

We may do it falteringly and without a deep
enough assurance, but we can lay hold of our heritage of renewed life and power. Christ definitely
bade us to do this. One who eats of the bread of
life consciously receives divine life, which cannot
grow old, frail, ineffective. One who drinks of the
water of life has that well of water springing up
within his own soul. He will not thirst again.

Even practical material science, leaving all mystic
experience out, now says that there is no reason
why man should not live in full vigor to at least a
hundred and fifty years. The body is constantly renewing itself unless we break the physical and
mental laws of well-being. Again we observe the
trinity that means perfection: the cheerful, courageous heart that gives forth good will; the uplifted
spirit that looks beyond the day, and the environ-

ment and the body keeping always the nice balance of activity, rest, and food. "But," you say, "no one has kept this law of proportion." Probably no one but Jesus Christ has; but there is the pattern. It is set for us. The goal is not an impossible one. We should be going toward it.

Our own experience with people close to us ought to teach us wisdom and application. Here are two people of the same number of years, perhaps in our own family. One is old, ailing, living in the past, letting go of all the interests of life. The other refuses to be old. He goes on with his work, he is always ready to extend a helping hand, he is inspiration to all about him. Look at these two closely, think over the roots of the difference, and then take the lesson home.

The race thought of age is not an abstract matter. We must do something about it today. Others have done something, and we must add our thought and effort to the growing store of good in this matter. Whether we are twenty-five or seventy-five as we read, it is our problem now. Each individual will suit his methods to his needs and his understanding, but there are some underlying principles.

Do not yield to suggestion or temptation to "retire." Keep working, not necessarily on the same job that you have been doing, but be sure you have a job that takes effort, makes you think, gives you responsibility, and above all, serves someone besides yourself. When you stop working, you are old. Body and mind begin to deteriorate, swiftly or slowly.

If you have already fallen into this error, come out of it today. It is not too late. It never is too late in God's time. Look about you now and find some service you can do for someone, some responsibility you can assume. It may seem very small, but never mind; it is only a beginning. Doors will open before you. There will be other things you can do, the vital things that mean new life. You will soon forget to count the years, to look for symptoms and aches and pains, to recount the losses and failures, to feel sorry for yourself and resentful of others.

In the "retirement" thought there are two errors, both springing from selfishness. The first is the desire to give up responsibility. Perhaps it has been ours long, and it is heavy. Someday we say: "Let someone else take it. I'm getting old. It's not expected of me. I'm going to give up all responsibility." When you say that, you have pronounced sentence upon yourself. Another retirement thought is that of ease. "I'm going to do just as I like. I'm going to be lazy and have a good time. I'm not going to have my declining years filled with effort and care. After all, I owe something to myself." Yes, we do indeed owe something to ourselves, but that is not the debt. Shun these two pitfalls.

Keep your zest in life. How long since you

have stood outdoors on a chilly evening and looked up at the stars, saying with David, "The heavens declare the glory of God." You used to take a walk in the woods in early spring while snow was yet on the ground to see if the skunk cabbage was out. A little later you went to scrape away dead leaves and kneel over the beauty of the arbutus. You knew almost to a day when the first anemones, the earliest wake-robins would be out. How long since you have taken a trip of exploration to the woods? Have you dared to say, "I'm too old to be wandering around over rough ground"? How long since you have really looked at a sunrise or a sunset? Do you still listen for the cardinal's song of "What cheer"?

But we must keep our zest for more than the miracles of nature. Are we moved when we hear of the hungry, the dispossessed left in the bitter wake of war, moved enough to do something about it? That is far away, and perhaps we send our boxes of clothing and food, and even write letters to some foreign friend to whom we have reached out over the seas. But we must live to the full in our own neighborhoods and families. That takes more grace of spirit.

There is that moody grandchild struggling up over handicaps we know well. Can we do something for him, not by censuring or urging but by making a quiet spot in our own home where he may come and rest, feeling sure of understanding? What about the wayward niece reaching out so greedily for the pleasures that she thinks are the end of life? What about the gifted but inarticulate neighbor who is rather pushed about by his own family? There is someone near and dear to us who needs understanding and sustaining love. Let us not fail here.

Get a job. What job? If you ask in sincerity you will find the job staring you in the face. If you do not need to earn money thank God for that added freedom, and take a job that is paid in the divine coin of the multiplied returns for what has been given out.

Keep faith strong and alert. As the years pass our faith should keep growing stronger because we put it to daily use. But once in a while we meet someone who says: "My faith is about gone. All of the ships I launched have come drifting home with empty hulls and broken sails. I can't believe in God's love and good will for us puny humans that clutter up this wandering planet." That is old age. But the eternal youth sees with the clear inner vision and knows that a Father's love infolds us.

Dwell consciously in the presence of God.

"Still, still with Thee when purple morning breaketh,
    When the bird waketh and the shadows flee;
Fairer than morning, lovelier than the daylight,
    Comes the sweet consciousness, I am with Thee."

Thus the New England poet tells of her security in the words of a hymn. We too, may have this.

God is already here. All we need is to be aware of it. It is as simple as repeating a few words of affirmation again and again just to remind us. Dwell in His presence. There can be no old age, no withering away of the powers of mind and body in that presence. Where God is there can be no error, failure, disappointment, sickness, or death.

And if some happy morning a door opens before us, giving us a glimpse of beauty not to be measured in words, and we hear a voice long familiar saying, "Come with me to a higher place," how gladly we shall reach out a hand unafraid and go with the sure Guide into the next experience of life. For there is no death.

FOR MEDITATION

I deny all thought of old age or failure; I lay hold on renewed life and power, through Christ in me.

—*Elinor Heath.*

The Kingdom of Right Relationships

T HE PARABLE of the unforgiving servant was related by Jesus in answer to a question, as so often was His custom. Peter asked Him: "Lord, how oft shall my brother sin against me, and I forgive him? until seven times?" It might seem that Peter was showing off just a little. The people in Jesus' company knew that the Old Testament law had always been "an eye for an eye, and a tooth for a tooth," but Peter had absorbed the Master's teachings and was willing to forgive "until seven times" if necessary! But Peter's ego was soon to be deflated. "I say not unto thee, Until seven times; but, Until seventy times seven." Then Jesus sketched the vivid picture of the unforgiving servant, to illustrate his point.

The first thing to do in our study of this parable is to remove it from the realm of money. It is evident that Jesus intended this, for the sums of money used in His story are fantastic figures. A servant "owed him ten thousand talents." Such a sum would have perhaps paid all the taxes in a dozen or more provinces. One can almost imagine His audience chuckling at such a pointed exaggeration. But Jesus wished to draw a very striking picture of this servant who, after having been completely forgiven this enormous sum, went out and cast into prison a man who owed him but "a hundred shillings."

Thus we see that this parable illustrates the relationships between God and man and between man and his fellow man. In His use of exaggerated comparisons Jesus pointed out that man could never possibly repay God. If he were to give every moment of every day for years and years he still could not repay God, who is constantly and lovingly forgiving him for whatever he has done. We must remember that in both the Lord's Prayer and in His other teachings Jesus stressed forgiveness: in order to deserve and receive forgiveness the only condition required of man is that he always be ready and willing to forgive his fellow man. Forgiveness of our shortcomings is not an experience that takes place in our hearts alone, but rather in our hearts and the hearts of those whom we think have wronged or hurt us. This is implied every time we say the Lord's Prayer. He who will not forgive another shuts himself away from God's forgiveness and that broken relationship has to be restored. "If therefore thou art offering thy gift at the altar, and there rememberest that thy brother hath aught against thee [not that you have something against him!], leave there thy gift before the altar . . . first be reconciled to thy brother, and then come and offer thy gift." Lord Herbert once said, "He that cannot forgive others, breaks the bridge over which he himself must pass." There can be no private relationship with God. His kingdom is a community where love and forgiveness between all men are essential.

So we see that in reality forgiveness is the restoration of a relationship, and this must be as complete as if the relationship had never been broken. This forgiveness must not be condescension, which merely builds up our egotism and sense of self-righteousness. It must be a loving, sincere response from the Christ within us to the Christ within the other person. We must say in our heart: "From this moment I do not think of you as a human being with human faults and failings any more than I wish others to think of my human frailties. The Christ in you can never hurt or disturb the Christ in me. The Christ in me can never be hurt, or resentful, can never feel a grievance, or be unforgiving. I will see only the truth as God sees it in you and in me." Such is the forgiveness of the heavenly kingdom.

Perhaps there is a letter you need to write. Is it one of explanation? One of apology? One of forgiveness? Or one of good will and friendship? Do not put it off! Never mind the probable response. Leave that in God's hands. The important thing is for you to write your letter. "Every one therefore that heareth these words of mine, and doeth them, shall be likened unto a wise man." The sense of relief, the wholesome self-respect that you will experience will be rewarding. Besides, it will be beneficial to your mental and physical health. The barrier that was holding your good from flowing through from the Spirit of all good will have been removed, and you will be greatly blessed.

The servant in the parable thought he would gain by holding on to his resentment, his sense of having been badly used, and his righteous wrath. Jesus shows clearly the blind folly of such thinking, the dense ingratitude of it. God constantly and freely forgives man, but man *receives* this forgiveness only *when* he loves and forgives. The measure of forgiveness received from God's hands and the measure of consequent love felt and acted upon by man are in direct ratio; such is the law of the kingdom. First there must be a conscious need for forgiveness and then a willingness to forgive. The servant, once he left his master's presence, felt no need for forgiveness. He possessed no sense of deep humility. Humility and gratitude prompt the heart to forgive and forget all hurts, all grudges, and all grievances.

Let us remember to be grateful every moment of every day. One's heart cannot be filled with gratitude and resentment at the same time. It would be impossible. For many years, a woman of my acquaintance had felt a great bitterness toward another whom she held partially responsible for the death of her sister. Resentment had soured this woman's normally pleasant disposition. Then Unity teachings were brought to her attention, and she began to learn the true meaning of forgiving love. Slowly the seed of forgiveness took root and began to grow, displacing the unlovely weed of resentment. Today resentment is gone, and my friend is one of the sweetest women I know. Powerful and splendid are the ways of Truth; soft but insistent are the stirrings of angel wings in our hearts, telling us to be big enough and wise enough to forgive freely and fully.

FOR MEDITATION

Dear Father, help us to be so grateful to Thee for Thy forgiving love that we may hold no grudge, no hurt, no anger. Help us to forgive our debtors as You are always forgiving us. Help us to see and love and respect the Christ in our fellow man. Help us to be generous in mind, in heart, and in soul. In the name of Jesus Christ. Amen.

—Kathleen W. Welch.

For the Joy Set Before Him

"I DON'T WANT any of that," said our son when dessert was brought on.

He didn't want any—and it was his favorite dessert!

But he went on to explain, "I'm on the training table at school, and we aren't allowed any rich desserts."

You might expect that a healthy sixteen-year-old boy would make this announcement sadly. For several months he was to watch his diet and refuse many things he liked. At school the choices were made for him, and he ate at a special table, but during the week ends at home he must exercise self-control and continue to follow the school rules.

Anyone who knows a boy who has won a place on the school team will assure you that he isn't sad because of the restrictions he must obey. He does not look for chances to escape the hard disciplines; he glories in them. Our boy's voice rang with pride as he told why he did not take his favorite dessert. Throughout the football season he kept the rules that the coach had laid down.

We usually think that our children rebel against discipline, but perhaps we need to reconsider. It is true that most of our "do's" and "don'ts" meet with resistance. The children want to do as they like, not as we think best. Discipline is a heavy yoke; yet there are times when discipline is accepted gladly by a young person—"for the joy" that is "set before him."

Can it be that there is something wrong with our discipline when the child feels that it is heavy and serves no purpose except to deprive him of pleasure? Have we failed to set before him the joy that is the fruit of all wise discipline? For there is no lasting joy in life without discipline, nor is there any worth-while achievement without it. Good habits cannot be formed without it; good health depends upon it.

Every minister, teacher, and counselor meets with the undisciplined adult often. Here is the woman who is overweight, without energy, suffering from headaches, but she assures the teacher that she eats three square meals a day. Well—yes, and she sometimes takes a snack between meals. She wants counsel and especially prayers from others that her health may be improved. What can be said to her? "Sin no more." That is what Jesus said to some of those whom He healed but who, He saw clearly, were on their way to more disease and pain.

"Sin no more, lest a worse thing befall thee." This is the injunction that many sick people need today. But if it is even suggested to them they will indignantly say that they do not sin. They never tell lies and do not slander their neighbors. They are honest in all their dealings, and they help wherever they can. All this may be true. Many self-indulgent people are honorable and kind, but nevertheless they go on breaking the physical and mental laws day after day.

We need to give this matter of discipline of the whole being more careful thought. The physical laws too are God's laws. The God who set holiness before us as a pattern for the spirit likewise set wholeness before us as a pattern for the body. We cannot put up fences and divide man's nature into physical, mental, and spiritual parts. There is no such division. Mind and spirit act upon the body, and body and mind act upon the spirit. There is no health for one part while the other parts are breaking the law and wandering in ways of sickness and confusion.

Suppose we set before our eyes the goal of perfect health of the whole being. Truly that is a joy set before us. But we do not get it by just wishing for it. No, nor do we get it by praying for it unless our prayer is more than the mere saying of words, the making of an appeal. We must keep the whole law; we must bring our will into accord with the Father's will. We must accept discipline gladly, looking upon it as an evidence of the Father's care for us. We must not fear it, nor obstinately refuse it. Like the schoolboy, let us learn to accept it gladly. Is today's way hard for us? There are reserves of strength within us, as we need them, and when we have risen above today's difficulty we have more wisdom and strength for overcoming the difficulties of the morrow.

The apostle Paul said in his second letter to young Timothy: "God gave us not a spirit of fearfulness; but of power and love and discipline." Power and love are not enough. Without discipline they may hinder rather than help us in gaining life's fulfillment.

We have considered those who need discipline because they give way to appetite. Let us consider another class, different but large, who are undisciplined in mind. Here is the clock watcher. It would seem that his only interest in his job is to see how soon he can get it over with and get away. He has probably been undisciplined from childhood. He has an untrained child's feeling that work is something to be avoided. He has not been taught by others nor by himself that work is a privilege, that good work is a glory—any kind of good work— that as we serve our fellow men in good work we are directly serving the Christ.

This man's oft-expressed wish is that he may come into a large sum of money (without working for it), so that he can give up work. Experience, observation, and history combine to tell him that only the good worker comes into the abundant life. He wants better wages, promotion, a position with more prestige. Here are joys set before him that can be won only by good work. But he grumbles at the disciplines that would make him a good worker.

It will require a mental revolution to make him take an interest in his work and become a good worker.

What are the disciplines that will train us for effective living? Let us discard forever the pagan idea that God inflicts upon us some arbitrary punishment because we have not obeyed His will. God does not give us a beating by sending us bodily pains. He does not cause us to lose our property, saying, "Now see what I do to you because of your sins and failures." In all our searching of Jesus Christ's teaching about the Father we find no indication of a God like that. Jesus Christ spoke the sure word. He knew because He and the Father were one. He said in forthright words: "God so loved the world, that he gave his only begotten Son." He told the parables of the prodigal son and of the good shepherd who sought the lost sheep, to tell us in our own language what God is like.

Punishment is not discipline, nor does it reform. We do not become better within because some stronger person has inflicted pain from the outside. But while God does not punish arbitrarily, by inflicting some unrelated punishment, the eternal laws of God do carry the penalty within them. The punishment is the result of the sin against the law. For example, Truth is the eternal law. By plain teaching and by perpetual example we are warned that man must not trifle with Truth. Then we see that the liar is continually more distrusted. In everyday life he may lose his job, lose his friends, lose any influence he may have had; and if he persists in breaking the law of Truth, he will lose even his ability to distinguish between truth and falsehood. We might similarly follow through the errors of selfishness, of indolence, of shirking responsibility, or of hate. But they all add up to the total that God's will to His children is good, and the eternal laws are designed for their advantage in all realms of life. Pain and loss come upon us because the race has wandered so far from the Father's will of good. The laws God laid down for His world are the only ones that will work. When we depart from them we hurt ourselves and others.

Here is a child in a home where he is surrounded by love and safeguarded by wise parents. He goes to play on the railroad track, though he knows that it is forbidden. If he fails to see the switch engine in time he is injured. The parents rush to help him. All that man's wisdom has gathered of the art of healing is called in to help restore him. Though he has sinned, and hence been hurt, he is not outside love. When he gets well the law is still there that children must not play on the tracks. But he will never again need to be reminded by parents. His mentor is now within. So we older children who may have wandered and been hurt by loss, failure, confusion, and sickness are never outside God's love. We may come back when we will. And when we have turned in true repentance to the Father our discipline will be from within.

Rules may be made from the outside, and we may obey them because we fear the result of breaking them; but until we accept them because they lead to something we desire they do not make us wiser and stronger. Any lad recruited for service to his country will soon learn to obey the rules in basic training. But the one who has the makings of a good soldier will see what the rules are for, and he will obey them whether an officer's eyes are upon him or not.

The good citizen of a country wishes to defend her even with his life. He chooses to keep the laws. He organizes his life in co-operation with his brothers, who likewise desire the good of all. "When all men's good is each man's aim" is a brief statement of his goal. Or better yet as Jesus Christ defined it when He summed up the two basic commandments: "Thou shalt love the Lord thy God with all thy heart" and "Thou shalt love thy neighbor as thyself."

Thus we see first of all that discipline is acceptable because it is the way to something we deeply desire. If we see the joy that is set before us we do not need the outside authority nor the fear of punishment to make us keep the law. We are our own policeman, and we never transgress. The divine law is in our heart.

"His delight is in the law of Jehovah;

And on his law doth he meditate day and night," said the Psalmist of the man who understood this. His conclusion is "Whatsoever he doeth shall prosper."

Can we know just what discipline is needed by us to strengthen us at our weak points, to help us overcome our straying tendencies, to help us fix our mind on the worth-while goal, to help us come fully into the divine plan? Yes, it is all written in the directions that Jesus Christ left for His brothers on earth. No two persons will need the same practice, but everyone can fashion his own discipline from the broad general directions.

When we seek discipline for health let us remember that by health we mean health of the whole being. It is not enough to have a strong body and a lazy mind. To have a keen mind and low desires is to turn away from real health. To ask for holiness in spirit and not ask for wholeness of mind and body is to make an incomplete prayer, far short of what Jesus Christ held up as our pattern. Sometimes we read of saints who ignored the body or even abused it. As we try to understand God's will today we do not believe that is His way. They would have been greater conquering saints if they had sought wholeness for the body too. So we, following the Way, in humility and faith ask wholeness for body, soul, and spirit.

To attain wholeness we must begin early practice in the disciplines for health. "In nothing too much" is a very old Chinese admonition. Consider how sound it is. Most of our suffering comes from "too much." When we have too much food, too much ease, too much play, too much money, too much concern for self, the body and the mind begin to deteriorate. If we accept the discipline of good physical and mental habits we stop this drain upon the good health that God decreed as our portion. Remember we are to control, not deny, the normal urges of life.

In talking of discipline for education we are not thinking only of the discipline of the schools. They do discipline us, but real education comes from life. We learn from the things formally taught us by instructors, from our reading, from history, from the events passing before us, from what happens to others who have kept or not kept the divine law, and most of all from experience. Can we relate what happens to us, to the causes that we have set in motion? Animals can learn from one sharp lesson of bad results. A young puppy in the country will chase the first skunk he sees—but never again. He has had one lesson, and he doesn't need a second one. But some of us human beings are much slower to learn. We have to be burned again and again before it sinks into our mind that fire burns. If we are to be fully educated we must accept the discipline of learning from observation and experience.

In disciplining ourselves for creative work we must seek first to remain active. After we have passed the playtime of childhood, inertia seems to dog our footsteps. Why keep on trying for what we may never achieve? If we have found a reasonably secure place, why not settle down in it, without trying for some visioned higher good? We say that life's pathway is all strewn with failures and disappointments. But we sons of God must not give up before these grim specters.

The child in school has days when most of his answers to problems are wrong. He is in despair. He feels that he will never master arithmetic. But do we let him drop out of school at this point and live without training for the difficulties ahead of him? We do not. Perhaps we help him straighten out the problems; we tell him that he may do better tomorrow. We assure him that arithmetic must be mastered, else he will not be able to do algebra when he comes to it. Certainly he must keep on going to school, and we exhort him to gird himself with courage and study harder so that there may be no more days of failure.

Yes, we are very sensible about the child and his school failures. But we forget that we are in school too, and some of us refuse to accept the discipline of today's failure. It should be a preparation for greater strength and wisdom tomorrow. If we are good students we shall perhaps after a while come to the day when we have a perfect grade, and we hear the Master's commendation: "Well done."

Finally we need discipline in the law of love. Have we been so shortsighted as to think that there is no discipline in love? Love's discipline is the sternest of all—not the hardest to accept, but the most exacting. Have you never seen a young girl make herself over to meet the ideal of the youth with whom she has fallen in love? A rough young man will become gentle and considerate for the sake of the maiden he hopes to win. A mother who has been an irresponsible girl will become steadfast and strong when there is a little child to be nurtured. A friend will develop unsuspected resources when his friend needs help.

These disciplines which we take so gladly to ourselves make us set high standards for others. The one we love is not indulged and spoiled. He is held to the disciplines of a high standard. So we accept Jesus Christ's law for our highest discipline: "Love the Lord thy God with all thy heart, and . . . thy neighbor as thyself." This rules out every conflicting and disruptive thing. In the acceptance of this happy discipline we go on over life's barriers.

FOR MEDITATION

I discipline my physical self, that I may better express my spiritual self.

—Zelia M. Walters.

You Are Persistent

G OD never gives up or gets tired.
God is life, and His life is ever expressing itself through many forms of manifestation. Life is everywhere present in our visible world,
and it manifests itself through plants, animals, and
man. If winter stops the growth of plants for a time,
they burst forth at the first opportunity for growth
in the spring. Life is always awaiting an opportunity
for expression.

God does not give up His work and cease to
supply life, love, or wisdom to His universe at any
time.

Since God is not a quitter, you, His child, are
not a quitter either. I see you in Spirit as you really
are, untiring, resolute, persistent, and undaunted. I
see you surmounting all obstacles. Even when you
sometimes seem to fail you pick yourself up and
with renewed energy press onward to the goal of
your high calling.

You are not subject to discouragement, because
you are impelled by an inner urge that carries you
on to victory. Because the Spirit of God is with you,
you cannot fail in any righteous undertaking.

You do not lose interest in what you are doing.
You cannot be wishy-washy or unstable, because you
are firmly established in the consciousness of pure
principle, which does not change.

You are persistent, firm, and unwavering in principle, yet you are open-minded, tolerant, and flexible enough to change your thoughts, words, or acts when you see that they can better conform to the principles of Spirit. You are not bound by personal consciousness or by preconceived ideas of right and wrong, but you are upheld by the principle of righteousness. The human part of you is flexible enough to adjust itself daily if necessary in order to conform more nearly to principle. Your watchword is "Not my will, but thine, be done."

Truth never changes. Principle never changes; but the application of principle is varied. In applying principle to any task you are steadfast; you are persistent; you do not give up, yet because you are flexible and open-minded, you see your task from all sides.

You are not limited to one dogmatic outlook. You do not look at the elephant's tail and insist that the elephant is like a rope all over, as one of the blind men in the old fable did. You do not take hold of the elephant's leg and say the elephant is like a tree, nor do you merely pat his side and say he is like a wall. You look all over your elephant problem; you look at his legs, tail, sides, trunk, and ears, and you see him as a whole. You study each task from all angles until you have discovered the secret of doing it the best way.

You easily overcome the inertia of human aversion to persistent effort by your steadfastness in the spirit of persistence. You are lifting up your human self, making it more and more like its perfect pattern in Spirit, the Christ in you. The Christ does not change in Spirit, yet Jesus, who most perfectly embodied the Christ, forgave His enemies, visited sinners, and submitted to the laws of the land.

You are a tower of strength because your strength abides in God. You are blessed and prospered in your faithful remembrance of divine resources.

FOR MEDITATION

I persist in the good, with a glad faith that God blesses me in it.

—*Lowell Fillmore.*

To a Lonely Heart

IF YOU feel lonely it is because you have a great undeveloped capacity within you that is calling for expression. Therefore do not be sad, but rejoice. Do not dwell upon the negative aspect of this undeveloped capacity and feel sorry for yourself, but instead look for a way to make use of it. Your loneliness may now seem to be a liability but you can turn it into an asset that will bring you much joy, success, and happiness.

Think of your loneliness as an empty boat that you are rowing among many struggling people in the water who are reaching out to you for help. You are sad because you are alone in the boat. Why not share your boat with those who need your help? Your boat represents your capacity to love people.

You have a big heart capable of holding much love. This is capacity, but capacity must be filled with something. A big grain elevator is good but it should be full of grain. An electric generator is good but it should not stand idle.

God has placed within you a great yearning to appropriate and use more of His love, His power, His life. Realize that the loneliness that you feel is a soul hunger for more of God's love. Because this soul hunger comes from God it is a blessing. You can promote the process of appropriating more of God's love by giving thanks to Him for His love even before you feel it. Bless your loneliness and thank Him for giving you such a great capacity for receiving and giving out His love.

You may have thought that you must first receive love from other persons before you can love them, but God has already given you His love in abundance and therefore you have an abundance to give. "We love, because he first loved us." Begin today to radiate the love God has given you and you will start the circuit of giving and receiving, and as a result you will experience more love and happiness than you ever dreamed could be crowded into your life.

Realize that it is really God that you are yearning for and not mere personal friendship. When you love God you will not want for friends. Therefore open your soul with thanksgiving to the realization that God is truly closer to you "than breathing, and nearer than hands and feet." But you must begin expressing the God qualities that are already in you if you would get their benefits.

Remember that Jesus Christ said, "Lo, I am with you always." God acting through His perfect Son, the Christ, is with us always. How can anyone be lonely when he realizes that the Christ of God is with him always?

When we seek first for the kingdom of God then all things needful will be added to our store of good things. It may be stated thus: "Seek first the kingdom of God and a host of friends will be added."

Many persons crave human friendship, praying that others may be friendly, when their greatest need is to express the love and friendship that is already within their heart.

Loneliness cannot be overcome by getting something; it must be remedied by giving something. The world is searching for men who have positive faith in God's living presence, who have living faith in His omnipresent love and power. Such persons are magnets that draw to them many souls who are seeking for God. Those who have not yet strengthened their faith in God feel that they must find God through some personality. A person like you could be of great help to many of these little ones by helping them find God for themselves. Your association with such as these would be a true remedy for your loneliness.

You can be of great service to God and mankind by showing many who are of uncertain faith the way to find fellowship with God within themselves. Thus you can develop a new appreciation of friendship and never again know the negative side of loneliness. You will then realize that your loneliness was only an unsatisfied hunger or need for expression and not a human wail for coddling, flattery, pity, and personal attention. God in you is the answer to all your needs: not God in the other fellow.

"The only way to have a friend is to be one." This is one way of saying, "Use the friendly powers that God has given you and you will find a response to them in other people." Do not bottle up your friendly feelings and wait for someone to come along and uncork the bottle. Loneliness is friendship in reverse.

There may be someone who is lonely; in fact there are doubtless many who are lonely in your vicinity, waiting for someone to come and cheer them up. How can you and they get together to have a mutual cheering up if each sits back and waits for someone else to start? I suggest that you fill yourself so full of God's love and good will that you cannot help showing by your every thought, word, and action the joy of fellowship. Friendship and good will begin in the heart and then transform the world without. This is the law of expression and growth.

The lonely heart is a big, loving heart locked up in a mental prison where it cannot express itself. All the wonderful energy, opportunities, and possibilities are turned earthward toward the self instead of heavenward toward God. As soon as love is turned toward God its mighty power begins to unfold and expand, transforming one's whole life and all one's association.

For Meditation

Blessed is my soul hunger for friendship, for it is being filled with the satisfying substance of God's love.

—*Lowell Fillmore.*

Thanks unto Jehovah

All thy works shall give thanks unto thee, O Jehovah;
And thy saints shall bless thee.
They shall speak of the glory of thy kingdom,
And talk of thy power.

* * *

Enter into his gates with thanksgiving,
And into his courts with praise:
Give thanks unto him, and bless his name.

YOU WILL OBSERVE, if you study the Scriptures in the light of Spirit, that those wise prophets who bore testimony to God's inspiration always gave thanks. Their thanksgiving may not be couched in just the terms that we would use, but the wise ones express recognition and gratitude and a devout thanksgiving for the good, even before it is received. There was going forth from the heart of the devotee the spirit of thanksgiving for wisdom, for the things of daily need, and, in the case of Jesus, for the ever-present Father of power and support. The highest form of prayer is affirmation of that which is in Being. It is praise of the good. Praise the peace of your own inner self. Rejoice and be glad in the actual possession of that Holy City within, and its gates will swing open to your inner eye, and its peace will pervade your whole consciousness.

Tradespeople have found that thank-you has a commercial value, and it is being used widely in the business world. Metaphysicians find that words which express thanks, gratitude, and praise release latent energies of mind and spirit, and their use is usually followed by pronounced effects.

Let your words of praise and thanksgiving be to Spirit, and the increase will be even greater than it is when addressed to man. The resources of Spirit are beyond our highest flights of imagination. You may praise a weak body into strength; a fearful heart into peace and trust; shattered nerves into poise and power; a failing business into prosperity and success; want and insufficiency into supply and support.

If you wish to know about a certain thing and believe in the great, everywhere-present Mind as the source of all knowledge, go into your "secret place," the deep recesses of your mind, and begin at once to give thanks to God that you *do* know. Praise the Mind of wisdom and understanding—exalt your understanding and the one Presence through your word; and in some way, through a vision or a dream or a flash of spiritual discernment, you will receive the knowledge you are seeking.

This law has been used by wise men all down the ages, but few have attempted to explain it. However, it is not hard to understand that mind synchronizes with mind, like the blending of music, when a keynote has been struck. When you have considered the matter in the light of Spirit and given thanks for its consummation, you have fulfilled the most potent, yet the most simple of all laws. It is the law of mind action, and it always proves itself. How important it is that we take advantage of it. Neglecting it, we see why we have fallen short in some of our demonstrations. As a nation, we give thanks to God on but one day out of the year. We are not commanded to give thanks even then. In the year 1863, President Lincoln suggested that the nation follow the precedent given us by the Pilgrim Fathers in 1623, and have a yearly day of thanksgiving—giving thanks especially for an abundant harvest. It is quite perfunctory in spirit, and no one has expected or observed special results. We should not look for great results from one day's thanksgiving out of three hundred sixty-five. Thanksgiving does not depend upon the President's proclamation. Neither is it fulfilled by ceasing to chase dollars for one day out of the year.

Thanksgiving must be something more than mere cessation from one's daily work. All the feast days in the old Levitical law—giving thanks to God for the escape from Egypt, for the passing through the Red Sea, and the entering into the Promised Land— had a deep meaning to the Jewish people. It was not the eating and drinking at the feast, but the prayer and supplication and thanksgiving to God that moved them. Through obedience, they came into possession of a law that lies at the very foundation of all true prosperity. Thanksgiving is accumulative.

True thanksgiving is the soul's recognition of its re-
lation to God, and there is no limit to its capacity.
Jesus, in His parable of the talents, taught that the
one who used his talent was commended by his lord,
while the one who buried his talent was condemned.

Do you think Jesus advised getting ahead of others by tricky competition or heartless oppression?
No. He knew the value of knowledge in lessening
the burdens of the oppressed. If men were possessed
of larger wisdom, they would have greater possessions.

There is a spirit of finance. There is a spirit of
accumulation, and an aberration of dissipation also.
These are thought atmospheres that work in the
minds of men and are carried along by the race.
Jesus came as the master manipulator of these
thought atmospheres. He told us to get away from
the mere material—in effect, to rise up into the
psychological; to take advantage of mental and
spiritual law. Jesus knew that the spiritually wise
should be above the materially wise, yet without
guile. "Be ye therefore wise as serpents, and harm-
less as doves."

Everything increases when it is praised. This is
a law of mind action. If you give thanks in the
spirit of generosity—seeing abundance for everybody—the law works for you. But you must forgive
men their debts. Jesus commended the steward who
cut in half the sums owed to the landlord. "Owe
no man anything, save to love one another," said

Paul. Debt is to be forgiven in the kingdom of God. In their great thanksgiving feasts, the Jews forgave all debts. This is prophetic of the Golden Age to come, when debt and usury and taxes will be wiped away.

The limitations of the realm of appearances stand in the way of those who do not know this great law of increase through praise and thanksgiving. When Jesus was informed that the multitudes which followed Him into the wilderness were hungry, He asked what they had. The answer was, "We have here but five loaves, and two fishes." This was so inadequate to the feeding of five thousand people that the apostles would not consider it; but Jesus said, "Bring them hither to me." "And he took the five loaves, and the two fishes, and looking up to heaven, he blessed, and brake and gave the loaves to the disciples, and the disciples to the multitudes." They were all fed and had twelve basketfuls left over. The central idea in this lesson is the power of the divine law to bring about large results from small beginnings when the increasing law of thanksgiving is set into action.

When you deal with spiritual forces, you should drop out of your mind all consideration of the meagerness of your faith. It is the little mustard seed of faith that will remove the mountain of materiality. Man must stimulate his mind with ideas of the presence and power of the omnipotent God. Then he will build up within himself the dynamic energy of the one life and the one substance until they overflow and increase everything he touches. This is not selfish accumulation of riches, but the demonstration of plenty for the multitudes.

This is a law that has its origin in mind, in ideas. Take into your mind ideas of the mightiness of God. He makes kings, and He unmakes them; He fixes the stars in the heavens; He makes the earth, and He fills it with His creations. Everything belongs to the Lord. Such thoughts will build up your appreciation of God as your resource. Then praise Him and give thanks to Him for all those things that you so greatly desire to be brought into manifestation, and it will be unto you "according to thy word."

FOR MEDITATION

I give thanks for the good I now have and for the good that I shall demonstrate henceforth.
—Charles Fillmore.

"What Is That to Thee"

I AM OFTEN amazed to discover how very human the Bible is, how very human the stories of Jesus and His disciples are. For a long time the thought "What *is that* to thee? follow thou me" has been one that I have used when I found myself becoming disturbed by situations that were really outside of my own province. When I looked up the words in the Bible I thought, "Why, Jesus used them in the same sense that I have been using them!"

Jesus was talking with Simon Peter about the work that lay before him, but Peter, the apostle John relates, "turning about, seeth the disciple whom Jesus loved . . . Peter therefore seeing him saith to Jesus, Lord, and what shall this man do? Jesus saith unto him, If I will that he tarry till I come, what *is that* to thee? follow thou me."

How often we are more concerned about what the other fellow is going to do than about what we know we should do. How often do we say, "But what about him?"

I grew up in a large family, and looking back, I wonder at the patience of my mother. I do not think she ever asked one of us to do something that we did not protest and ask why we had to do it if the others did not. "Why do I have to dry the dishes when Esther doesn't have to?" "Why

111

do I have to study? Ruth is going to a party." "Why do I have to eat my cereal? Priscilla didn't." And so on and on we went.

One of the most helpful lessons we can learn is to do what is before us to do without looking about to see what the other fellow is doing.

To learn to live our own life as well as we know how and to be willing to let the other person live his is one path to peace of mind.

It is really childish to fret about what another person does or does not do, especially if we let it keep us from accomplishing our own purposes.

Gossip is a cause of great inharmony and unhappiness in human relations; human beings are hurt and perhaps humiliated by some tale that is repeated and repeated about them.

If when we are tempted to pass along a piece of gossip we would stop and say to ourselves, "What is that to you?" we should find it easy to let the gossip die with us, to follow the Christ within, which is the very spirit of understanding and generosity and kindness itself.

Whether the gossip is true does not make any difference. It still is not our business to discuss unfavorably or unkindly another human being.

If every worker in every office could develop a "what-is-that-to-thee" state of mind, much inharmony and friction would automatically disappear. In many offices inharmony exists between the workers because everyone is minding everyone else's

business. A competent worker is not happy in his
work because the worker sitting at the next desk to
his fritters away the hours. A promotion is given a
person in the office, and the whole office force feels
resentful toward the person chosen for promotion.
A prompt worker resents the "ten-o'clock-scholar"
worker. A quiet worker resents the noisy worker; the
nonuser of the telephone resents the constant user
of the telephone. The "fresh-air fiend" resents the
worker with the closed-window habit. The worker
with every curl in place resents the breezes that blow
from the electric fan.

Now the person in charge of an office needs to
concern himself with such things, but as to the
rest, for all their worrying and fretting, for all their
criticism and condemnation, there is but one answer:
"What *is that* to thee? follow thou me."

If as children in a family we needed to learn
that our business was to do the thing before us
and not to worry about what the other children were
going to do, as adult members of a family we need
to learn this lesson even more. Many families are
so concerned with the actions of all of their members that there is no peace left for any of them.
"Why is she doing as she is?" "What made John
buy that big home, on *his* income?" "Why doesn't
Mary train her children better?" Grownups, yes, but
children still needing to learn to say, "What *is that*
to thee? follow thou me."

In-laws need to develop such an attitude even

more, for they are suddenly thrown together in a family relationship whether they like one another or not. I know a mother-in-law who really maintains an attitude of unconcern as to the actions and conduct of her sons-in-law and daughters-in-law, and she is one mother-in-law who is much loved. She said once, when someone was questioning her daughter-in-law's way of doing things, that if her daughter-in-law wanted to put her kitchen stove in the middle of the living room it was all right with her.

"What *is that* to thee? follow thou me." The last part of this statement is as important as the first, if not more so. If we were merely to shrug our shoulders mentally and say, "What is that to you?" we should be only half right. The clue to progress, to peace of mind, to happiness lies in the words "Follow thou me."

To follow the Christ is to follow the divine leadings from within, the promptings of Spirit that come to us when we pray, the divine instincts of love and compassion and understanding. To follow the Christ is to follow our highest self rather than our lesser self—our highest self, which is wise and forbearing, which is capable, which is victorious in all things. "Follow thou me" is the call of the great soul that we are in Truth; it is the call of the Christ within.

When we compare the things that disturb us and upset us with the power of the Christ within us we see them for what they are—nothing. We can say, "What is that to you?" and answer truthfully, "Nothing."

"What *is that* to thee? follow thou me."

FOR MEDITATION

I am not disturbed by what others do; I am serene and sure no matter what happens; I follow Thee.

—Martha Smock.

Our Divine Inheritance

NOT LONG AGO a woman with whom I was talking complained to me that although a practitioner had been working for her for two months there had not been the slightest improvement in her condition. "I have had this trouble since I was six years old," she said, and then added, shrugging her shoulders hopelessly, "Well, my father had it, and his brothers and sisters, his father's brothers and sisters. All their lives they suffered from this disease."

Throughout the world men and women are looking to their ancestors for their defects and talents, as most of the members of the human family have done through the ages. Heavy-laden with inherited ills are some; puffed up over inherited gifts are others. Slaves to the belief of human parentage, they wail and boast, while down through the centuries rings this command of Jesus:

"Call no man your father on the earth: for one is your father, *even* he who is in heaven."

Nothing involved or difficult to understand about that, is there? How very clear Jesus made it. Our Father, the only Father we have, is God, Spirit. We are not material but spiritual, the sons and daughters of God, of Spirit. "And if children, then heirs; heirs of God, and joint-heirs with Christ."

When the revelation that God is his true Father, the source of all good, is brought to man, the belief in good inherited from a human parent is given up and man sees that he inherited his good from his divine parent; that he has never inherited anything but good, and that from God. Awakening to the fact that "every good gift and every perfect gift is from above, coming down from the Father of lights," man frees himself from the belief of limited good and claims the unlimited good that his Father is forever pouring out for him. He begins to see the things that "eye hath not seen, nor ear heard." Undreamed of talents are revealed.

To most people, giving up the belief in human parentage means something heartless and cruel; a ruthless cutting off of all that is precious, of all that is lovely in one's life. But it means nothing of the sort. The gentlest, the most loving and most compassionate of men, the man whose love was so great that it embraced even those who hated Him, was He who said, "Call no man your father." His was not a binding love; rather it was a freeing love. And it is this freeing love, this true love, that man expresses for those who have served him in the human capacity of parents when he gives up the belief in human parentage. Releasing this false belief, he gains a right view of his earthly parents; he recognizes and honors their individuality. Like Jesus, he loves greatly, completely.

Jesus claimed God as His Father and proved His claim by His works. So must we. Jesus laid hold of the life and substance that were His divine heritage. We must lay hold of the life and substance that are our divine heritage.

God *is* our Father. To recognize this is to declare it in our every thought, word, and action. We *are* His heirs.

FOR MEDITATION

As a child of God I am a free spiritual being. I choose to express my Father's perfection.
                                        —*Marjory H. Stageman.*

The Greatest of These

"AND THE GREATEST of these is love," said Paul in his first letter to the Corinthians after enumerating a list of divine attributes. The accuracy of his statement becomes more and more clear to us as we continue to study and practice the teachings of Jesus Christ in our daily living. Love is indeed the greatest of all spiritual qualities, for it actually carries with it all the others.

Wisdom and understanding always go hand in hand with love. A noted philosopher once said, "Love all things, and you will soon know the mystery of all things." Yes, it is true that love unlocks the very secrets of the universe. The well-known American sculptor Dr. Walter Russell is a good example of this fact. He had only six grades of elementary schooling, and yet he has attained high honors in the fields of literature, art, and science. At the age of seventy-seven Doctor Russell is one of the world's greatest sculptors. His other achievements are outstanding. Doctor Russell said to the author: "Love of God and all His creations is one of the most important factors in the attainment of success and happiness. You can virtually love your way into the realm of cosmic knowing, and there all things shall be added unto you."

How can we best express or apply love in our daily living? How can we learn to love certain people or things that have hitherto been repugnant to us? These are the questions most often asked by those who earnestly desire to express God's divine love. The best way of course to apply love is to love. Love everything from the highest to the lowest, from the most beautiful to the ugliest, from the best to the worst.

If you find it difficult to love that which appears to be ugly, it is only because you do not understand it. If you desire to love that which is lowly, you already love it to a certain degree. Bless that which you would love, praise it, seek to know the truth about it, look for the good in it, look for God in it. He is there, you know. Once you fully realize this you will have no difficulty in loving the person or thing in mind. This process will eventually fill your heart with love toward all things.

Not long ago I was talking with two women, and during the course of our conversation the subject of bats came up. One of the women said that just to think of bats gave her "the creeps." She hates them intensely. The other woman has a feeling of compassion for such creatures, and she finds them interesting.

"I have handled bats and examined them closely," said the woman, "and you'd be surprised at how soft and velvety their wings are. Their fur is as silky as moleskin. And did you know bats have a regular radar system to keep them from bumping into things in the dark? God must love them a

lot to have given them such wonderful equipment.
I think they're wonderful little things."

Here is an excellent example of divine love. This
woman loves bats and other such creatures because
she looks for the good in them. She sees beauty
where others see ugliness. She loves that which others hate. She praises and blesses the lowly creature,
and to her it becomes beautiful. Through the power
of love this woman magnifies the beauty in everything she sees.

Another phase of our daily life in which the
spirit of love plays a most important part is our
occupation. Quite frequently I hear someone re-
mark: "I know it is important that I love my work,
but how can I? How can I love to do something that
is just a grind and drudgery to me?" It does seem
difficult sometimes to love the routine, but it can be
done in any instance, and it is amazing what happens
when we do learn to love our work. Here again it is
all a matter of attitude.

First of course you must desire to love your
work. Desire is the dynamo that sets in motion the
wheels of accomplishment. When accompanied by
faith and backed up by action, desire is the most
potent prayer man can express. If you really desire
then to love your work, begin to bless it. Give
thanks for the ability and for the opportunity to
do it. Do it as though it were God's work. Do it as
though He wants you to be doing it at the present
time. Do all to the glory of God.

I know a man who works almost constantly
with precision instruments. His tools are ever so
delicate, and the material he uses is sometimes ir-
replaceable. He has gained a wide reputation in his
field, and though his shop is quite small, he has
occasionally been called on by the government to
solve some intricate tooling problem. Knowing that
this man believes in the power of love and praise,
I asked him recently if he ever prayed while working in his shop.

"Yes," he said, "I feel very humble about my
work. I love my tools, and I frequently thank them
under my breath for the help they give me. It may
sound foolish, talking to inanimate objects like that,
but I firmly believe those tools respond to my praise
and blessing by turning out better work for me. Yes,
I love my work, and I thank God many times a day
for the ability He has given me."

If you really want to increase your love output,
get by yourself frequently in the silence and talk
to the people and things with which you are associ-
ated daily. Speak to them as though they were right
there with you. Say the words silently but sincerely:
"I love you in spite of your apparent shortcomings.
To me you are as perfect as the Father is perfect.
I love you, bless you, and pray for your highest
good. I love you because you are one with God and
one with me in the spirit of love. I love you because I cannot do otherwise. I thank God that I
love you." Say these words often and say them

sincerely; then go out and back them up with action.

Do not be afraid that thinking and speaking of love is an indication of weakness. It is anything but that. The power of love can win more battles for you than you could ever hope to win with your fists or with deadly weapons. Try it. Start living by the law of love today. Let love radiate from your heart as freely as light radiates from the sun. To love freely is to live fully. To restrict the flow of love is to restrict the flow of life. Man comes nearer to fulfilling his divine purpose when he expresses love than at any other time.

"Does this mean," you may ask, "that I am to love evil? Am I to love disreputable people and things that are opposed to God? Am I to love someone who hates me and tries to cause me harm?"

These questions bring up the great basic element in all Truth teaching, the allness of God. When you know the truth about God, that He is the only power and the only substance in the universe, you will not find it difficult to love people and things that appear to be evil. God loves them. He lets His blessed sun shine just as freely on those we call evil as He does on those we call good. To Him there is no evil. Only man recognizes evil. We frequently take God's good substance and place the label of "evil" on it; then we despise it and fret because it reacts accurately to the name we have given it. Love removes the label of evil and recognizes only the presence of God there. It eliminates undesirable elements and leaves only the eternal good.

While all the preceding aspects of love are important, the most important of all remains. "Thou shalt love Jehovah thy God with all thy heart, and with all thy soul, and with all thy might." This is the first commandment. It is not put before us however as a duty but rather as a glorious privilege. Love strengthens us in our relations with God by making our oneness with Him more obvious. It reveals the Father in His true nature. Most important of all though, our love for God enables us to accept His love for us. "Now abideth faith, hope, love, these three; and the greatest of these is love."

FOR MEDITATION

I love all people and all things, and God's love is poured out in my life.

—*Worral G. Sonastine.*

How to Make Your Work Easy

REMEMBER THAT ANY difficulty encountered in doing your work, whether that work is spiritual, mental, or physical, is usually due in a greater degree to your adverse attitude toward the work than to the character of the work itself.

There is an easy way and a hard way to do every job.

Approach a distasteful job in a friendly way, with interest, confidence, and enthusiasm, and it will become easy and pleasant. If on the other hand you dread the chore and fear it, or are uninterested in it, you will find it not so easy.

No one ever did a job very well or got much pleasure out of it who took the attitude that it could not be done. If you tackle a job without feeling any interest in it, or if you think it is not worth while, or if you are afraid of it, you will find it to be a hard job.

You can make a job more pleasant and easy if you will cultivate confidence in your ability to do it or at least to have faith that you can find a way to do it. Know that by the help of God you can discover a way and you will not fail. When you think of a way in which it might be done before you start to work you will open your consciousness to a trend of new ideas that will help you to do the job in a manner that will reflect credit upon you.

New ideas will flow into your mind when you clear the channel by exercising your faith in God's omnipresent wisdom. If you will spend a little time in silent prayer before you actually start working you will be ready to begin the work with joy and enthusiasm.

Before you do something that seems to be difficult say silently: "God goes before me, revealing clearly to me an easy and efficient way to proceed." And if this work requires some time to finish, become quiet a moment now and then while doing it, to let God show you the next step to take and to receive His blessing while you are at work.

All that you need to know about doing a job is already known to God, and He is ready and waiting to reveal this information to you as soon as you open the way with your faith. God is omniscient, and He will reveal a way to you when you have silenced the voice of your personal ego and are ready to listen to His still small voice.

The demands, opinions, ambitions, and whims of the personal ego shut out the voice of spiritual wisdom. When you have subdued your turbulent thoughts with the command "Peace, be still," you will be ready to receive wisdom from on high, and you will be amazed at the good ideas that God will reveal to you to aid you in making your work effective and interesting.

Every duty and every project that you undertake can be made easy and joyous if you will do it fearlessly to the glory of God. There is nothing too great or too small for God to help you with.

For Meditation

Infinite Wisdom, which knows all things, reveals to me the most efficient and pleasant way to do my work.

—*Lowell Fillmore.*

Thy Will

SUPPOSE YOU HAD a small boy in your home, say six or seven years old, who came home from school one afternoon clutching in his hand a piece of dirty candy that he had found in the street. Suppose he should announce that he was going to eat it for his supper instead of the wholesome food his mother had prepared for him with loving care. What would you do? What would you say?

Whatever your method of dealing with your child's ignorance and willfullness, what would be the basis of your efforts to prevent his hurting himself by indulging in a wish or a whim that was harmful to him? Your refusal to let him do as he liked would be based on your love for him and your desire to keep harm away from him and give him only what was good for him, would it not? You would know it was absurd for him to think he knew better than you did what was best for his health and happiness.

Did you ever come upon anything in your life whose taste seemed so sweet that you wanted it very much? Did you ever ask God to let you have it just because you wanted it? When apparently He denied it to you, did you make up your mind that you were going to have it anyway, because you could not understand that it might not be good for you?

Did you resent God's refusal to let you have this thing, revolt against Him because He would not give it to you, refuse the wholesome things He offered you instead, lose faith in His love because He did not grant your demand for it? Did you think you could know better than God does what is good for you?

Or have you lived long enough and grown up enough to learn that God always gives you what you really want and need, not perhaps exactly what you pray for in so many words but the fulfillment of the true desire in your heart, that which will be for your permanent well-being and happiness?

Jesus called God our Father in heaven because He wanted us to get a true conception of the loving wisdom and care God has for us. He intended us to understand that the love of earthly fathers and mothers for children exemplifies in a measure the infinite love of the Creator for His creatures. He gave us a model prayer in which He said to our Father, "Thy will be done," because He wants us to accept the will of infinite love as better than our own ignorant desire, and to surrender our determination to His superior purpose.

Doubtless you remember the story of the child who cried for the wasp on the windowpane, because it was "pretty." When his mother told him the wasp was dangerous and would hurt him, he grasped it anyway. It made him anything but happy when he got it. Are we like this child? Have we gained experience enough to know that when we grasp what we think we want, disregarding God's warnings and instructions, willful seizure brings us only pain and unhappiness?

I know a writer who thought he wanted a glittering job in Hollywood. There was nothing wrong about this, but the still small voice in him warned him that it was only the big salary he wanted and that the work would not satisfy his standards of workmanship or ideals. When the opportunity came the writer grasped the job, and it has made him miserable. Show business offers fine opportunities for some talents, but it is not a place for *his* talents. He finds himself disappointed, handicapped, frustrated.

A friend of mine drank himself to death because he thought the stimulation of liquor was what he wanted. What he really wanted was the inspiration that comes only from high purpose.

A man tells me he is praying for escape from an intolerable situation that has resulted from a wrong committed by himself. He does not realize that restitution (when it can be made by the wrongdoer) is an essential part of any real repentance that God will accept and that God forgives only the truly repentant.

If all such people prayed, "Thy will be done," and depended on God to give them supremely good answers, they would have no miseries and no doubts. In these four words is the one saving prayer.

Not that it is wrong to pray for things; it is right for us to have anything that harms no one, ourselves or anybody else. But would you not rather have what our Father knows you need than anything else whatever, even though it means discipline? God will give us what He knows we need, even if it takes a miracle. Jesus said, "seek ye first his kingdom, and his righteousness; and all these things shall be added unto you." Why then seek the things first and forget the kingdom?

Now I want to suggest a method that may help you very much. It is a well-established fact that relaxation and denial of appetite are among the best of all practices for promotion of bodily well-being. What is good for the body is good for the mind and spirit. Truth teachers too put relaxation first as an essential condition of spiritual experience. Get still is the simple rule; let go, the specific instruction. Let God is the all-covering precept. Let go. Let God.

All selfish desire involves strain; all self-assertion is indulgence of appetite. Jesus said: "If any man would come after me, let him deny himself." "Have faith in God." Jesus set the example in His life and in His oft-repeated prayer "Thy will be done" and in His whole attitude toward our Father. Do you not think He knew what brings peace —the condition of straight thinking and creative achievement? Do you not believe that He wanted us to find happiness?

Let us recall what some of our great sages have said about this. Shakespeare wrote,

"There is a divinity that shapes our ends,
Rough-hew them how we will."

Emerson said, "A little consideration of what takes place around us every day would show us that a higher law than that of our will regulates events; that our painful labors are very unnecessary and fruitless; that . . . by contenting ourselves with obedience we become divine." Jesus Himself told us, "Your Father knoweth what things ye have need of, before ye ask him"; and Isaiah records that God promised, "Before they call, I will answer." Our troubles and sorrows arise from our determination to have what we want now.

But God's will for us is not denial. His purpose is to teach us to use the power that moves mountains. He wants us to realize our own divinity. He wants us to live on high levels. He wants us to be not slaves but masters. He asks us to seek a kingdom, not a serfdom. His design is that life for us shall be not a frustration but a triumph. He wants us to have something better than we can imagine, more than we can ask or think. He offers us the desires of our heart.

God made everything. He knows where everything is, and what road leads to it. He knows what door opens to happiness. He knows what magnet attracts good. Why not let Him show us? Why not let Him give us His supreme gifts?

Why not let go and let God? It is the simplest and easiest thing we can do, and it brings the greatest rewards.

Hannah Smith, who wrote "The Christian's Secret of a Happy Life," says that the whole secret lies in surrender and trust, which means "abandonment" of self and absolute, complete reliance upon God. She compares this abandonment to lying down upon one's bed and surrendering to sleep. One has perfect relaxation, relaxation from willful determination into security, into trust in God. What I want to call your attention to is the well-known principle that relaxation of the body itself induces relaxation of the mind. Letting go of muscles induces the letting go of fears. Giving up strain induces the giving up of pain. These actions and reactions work in a benign circle; take hold of it anywhere and you have the whole, like an electric current you contact, like a view you can see, like a fruit you can pick, like a love you cherish.

If you find it hard to pray, "Thy will be done," try lying down on your bed and relaxing every fiber in your body. Just make a physical beginning. After you have made a beginning, relax a little more, and then a little more, until you yield completely and all strain ebbs out of you. It will occur to you to wonder, "To what am I yielding?" Your answer can only be that you are yielding to one of nature's laws that you do not understand, but one that you know brings you ease.

Presently you will remember that nature's laws
are God's laws, and it will occur to you that God
made His laws for the one and only simple purpose
of working for human good, and that He asks
only that you rely on His laws for help, and rest,
and peace, and fulfillment. God asks you to let go
to Him, to relax into His love, and to taste and see
that it is good. Soon you will begin to grasp the
great truth that the secret of a happy life lies in
letting go. The strains of desire and determination
and fear will ebb out of your mind and heart. Peace
will flow in—peace you cannot understand, peace
that passes all understanding. These thoughts in
some form will come to you.

Relax a little more, get still, and wait. The
still small voice will begin to tell you that you
cannot yield part of yourself to God without yielding the whole; that you cannot yield to a part of
God without yielding to the whole. You will know
you are touching reality. You will begin to understand that you are discovering God's will for you
and that it is infinitely better than your own will for
yourself. It will be easy then to pray the greatest
of all prayers, because you will have found the
greatest of your heart's desires. You will have
found the prayer that God answers before you
"call." The answer is already yours, while you "are
yet speaking."

Trying the letting-go method once will give you
a taste of peace and joy. After a first trial it will

be easier and simpler the next time. But when you have once surrendered, do not take yourself away from God. Let go more and more and again and again till it becomes a habit. Do not worry about your feelings; your decision is what counts. "I surrender, I trust; I know it is my open door to priceless good. Father, all I want is that Thy will be done."

Do not be afraid, only believe. Get up from your bed expectantly. Expect God to do His part. "I trust; God works. I expect; God fulfills. I have no responsibility for results; they are all in His hands." Affirm: "I seek the kingdom, and all things are added." "I delight also in the Lord, and He gives me the desires of my heart." "I have faith in God and according to my faith it will be done to me."

"Thine infinite good will for me and mine be done, in Jesus' name, and for His sake. I thank Thee that Thou hast heard me."

FOR MEDITATION

I deny my selfish desires; I let God's perfect desire be expressed through me.

—*Gardner Hunting.*

Your Right Leading

ARE YOU SEEKING GUIDANCE? Do you feel the need of help or light on some certain problem?

There is only one source of sure and dependable guidance, only one place to find real help and light. That place is within your own self.

If you sincerely and honestly follow the path that you feel in your heart is right, the path will lead you inevitably in the right way; you cannot go wrong. But you must follow it honestly, fearlessly, courageously.

It is more important to follow your sincere inner leading than it is to find the exact outer path to follow. For if you find the sincere inner leading and follow it, the right outer way will work itself out for you. It is a law of the universe that the outer follows the inner without fail.

Let me illustrate this cardinal principle in finding your right leading by using the experiences of Saul.

He believed that the teachings of Jesus of Nazareth were wrong. As an orthodox Jew, a Pharisee, he felt bound to do everything he could to stamp out this "upstart" religion or cult, which was contaminating Judaism.

Fired by his conviction, he persecuted Christians in every possible way and pressed his feeling

against them by acts of violence and by legal pros-
ecution. He followed his inner conviction with zeal
and, it must be said, with honesty.

On his way to Damascus to press action there
against the followers of Jesus, Saul had an experience that completely changed his mind. Instead of
a persecutor of Christians, he became an exponent of
the new belief.

As Paul, he followed his new leading with even
more zeal and enthusiasm than he had followed his
former leading. He had to face the same persecution
that he had meted out to others, yet he did not
flinch. He followed his inner conviction honestly
and fearlessly.

I am convinced that Paul's honesty in following
his original leading to persecute the Christians
caused him to be led into the right path of believing
in Christianity. Whenever anyone follows his inner
leading and conviction fearlessly and honestly, he
is unfailingly led into the right path.

How can *you* find your right leading in the
problem facing you? How can you find help and
guidance in the midst of confusion and conflicting
opinions and ideas?

Search your inner mind and heart in prayer and
earnest thought for the right leading. Ask yourself
the following questions:

*What do I really think and feel about the
matter?*

Setting aside all personalities and beliefs and conflicts with others, what do I think is right?

Regardless of the obstacles involved, which is the right path? Which will lead to the establishment of justice, righteousness, peace, and true principles in the world?

Aside from my own selfish desires and interests, what is right?

What do I think is right, measured by the principles and truths of God that I know?

If Jesus were talking with me about this matter, what would He tell me to do?

In answering these questions, search for sincerity of purpose instead of the right outer way. If you can achieve sincerity of purpose, the outer way will open in time.

Do not be greatly concerned about what someone else thinks is the best way. George Bernard Shaw said it brilliantly, if sharply: "If you do things merely because some other fool expects you to do them, and he expects you to do them because he thinks you expect him to expect you to do them, it will end in everybody doing what nobody wants to do, which is in my opinion a silly state of things."

Remember, only you can really decide the matter for yourself. Others may advise or help, but each person must know the right path for himself.

Once you have set out to find your right leading, have prayed about it and answered the purpose-searching questions, you will find a path taking form in your mind. There may seem to be a lot of obstacles, but your inner spirit of righteousness will show you what is right according to your principles. This is your right leading. You can have confidence in it and feel sure that God approves.

Did God approve of Saul's persecution of the Christians? God never approves of persecution and acts of violence, but He approved of the sincerity of purpose that moved Saul. Saul's sincerity of purpose led him into the right path.

As long as you follow your inner leadings honestly, God approves. And He will lead you into the right path just as surely as Saul was led.

You know that God looks upon the heart, not upon the outer man and his individual, separate, outer acts. These outer acts merely express the inner and will change when the inner man is changed. As long as you have sincerity of heart, God helps you to find the right outer paths.

What is it that keeps you from following this path or that? Is it not knowing for sure whether it is right? Well, you can know that it will lead you into the right path, if it is a leading that you have arrived at honestly. Should the outer aspect of it not be exactly right, you will be led into the right as you go along, if the inner heart is right. The outer follows the inner.

If two of you disagree as to the right path, which one is right? For you, only your own inner leading can be right. This is a very important point and one that causes many of us to get off the path of our inner leading. For your own practical purposes you must accept only your own inner leading. You must follow that. If the other person should turn out to be right, you will be led into his way naturally by following your own inner leading.

If you are right, the other person probably will come to know it by your living affirmation of it. But remember, your own inner leading is right for you, regardless of the beliefs or pressures of others.

As you go along you will have to overcome doubts, discouragements, and fears arising within yourself. No sooner do you start on a path than you are assailed by doubts. Take this rule as a safe one to follow: Once you have made up your mind, go ahead, until and unless you realize that the path is absolutely wrong.

If you have doubts, ask yourself, "Am I certain that I am following the wrong path, or am I only doubtful?"

If you are sure the path is wrong, then stop and follow your new leading. If you are only doubtful, dismiss the doubts by determining to follow the original course until you know absolutely that it is wrong.

A wrong path will soon show itself to be wrong when you start actually to follow it. Then you can correct the mistake and follow the right path. But indecision causes you to mark time.

If you become discouraged, force yourself to hold on a little longer and continue along the same path. After all, you can never work anything out by quitting.

Remember that as long as you let fear rule you, God cannot guide you. By the laws of its very nature, fear can lead you into nothing but worse conditions. But God can and will lead you into happiness and freedom.

Which do you want? Do you want to be a prisoner of your fears, or a free child of God?

Paul knew what was waiting for him if he chose to follow Christ. He knew because he had helped to inflict the very same treatment on others. Yet Paul did not turn back.

Almost everyone meets opposition when he tries to improve himself or make any changes in his life and affairs. Opposition must never be allowed to turn you from the right. After all, you can never establish the right by allowing the wrong to influence you. Paul met actual physical opposition more than once, but he did not turn from the path of Christianity.

Remember that your right leading can come only from you, not from anyone else. Look not to others for your right leading, but into your own heart and mind. Pick the path you sincerely feel is right; follow it. If it is not right, it will lead you into the one that is right.

Follow your honest inner leading in spite of

doubts, discouragements, fears, or opposition. This is the way to health, happiness, accomplishment, and peace of mind.

FOR MEDITATION

I search my mind and heart in prayer, and I do what God would have me do.

—*James E. Sweaney.*

Sensitive to the Good

AS A CHILD and as an adolescent I was very sensitive. As a woman I am still very sensitive —but I want to be sensitive now. No, not in the same way I was as a child, ashamed and humiliated, but in a brand-new way, a way that keeps me proud and inspired.

I often used to say, "I am so sensitive," which usually meant that I thought someone disliked me, had hurt, slighted, or misunderstood me. I suffered because I was sensitive. Now I rejoice because I am sensitive! Always I knew whether people liked me or not, and I felt it keenly if they did not. I still know ordinarily whether people like me or not, but I do not suffer if they do not. My thinking on the matter has been transformed.

What has brought about the difference in my sensitivity? I have the same sensitive nature with which I made my debut into the world. Why did I suffer once because of it, and why do I now value it and cultivate it?

It is not a matter of "Am I sensitive?" but "To what am I sensitive?"

I believe that a sensitive nature is a gift from God and that I should continually appreciate and cultivate it. But I should be careful how I cultivate it. One day when I was thinking about the statement, "God, the good, is all there really is," my mind jumped to this conclusion: "Then I will be sensitive only to the good!"

I am sensitive only to the good.

No more do I think that people dislike me, and never do I go home and cry over some unkind thing someone says about me or to me. I admit that making my emotions conform to my affirmation is not always easy. A habit of years seems to make a deep rut in the mind that is sometimes hard to avoid, but when I find myself slipping back into the habit of being sensitive to the negative idea I bless the one that I feel has hurt or slighted me. Thus I turn toward the things that are lively, true and "of good report," and my sensitive nature responds.

A friend of mine who always seems miraculously to find the good in every person and in every thing, who always has loads of sunshine to spread everywhere, told me with a twinkle in her eye about an experience she had had. One day her mother received a letter that upset and hurt her. When my friend got home she could see that her mother had been crying. She read the letter. The mother said, "Isn't it terrible?" In her philosophical way my friend replied, "Well, Mom, I don't think so; I can't see anything in it that need hurt you at all." Then she proceeded to read the letter again, this time aloud to her mother.

When she had finished it, the two women looked at each other for a moment. The mother always stretched her hands above her head whenever she laughed heartily. Now up went her hands and together mother and daughter laughed all the hurt and resentment away.

Most insults have their humorous side. We can see it if we look for it. Again it is not so much a question of "Am I sensitive?" but "To what am I sensitive?" It has been my privilege to help several people who have suffered as I did, because they did not know how to direct their sensitive nature toward happiness.

Every day there are things that I could let hurt and disturb me, and I could excuse myself by saying, "I am so sensitive." No doubt it would net me some sympathy and I could wallow in tears and self-pity, but there is a better way, a way that nets me understanding, laughs, self-assurance, a way that is all wrapped up in one little sentence: "I am sensitive only to the good."

FOR MEDITATION

I know that the adjusting power of God is working mightily in my life. I am sensitive only to His good.

—Blanche Tromblé Evans.

How Are We Praying?

How are we praying? Do we know how to pray? God always answers prayer, if we believe our prayer. Jesus said: "All things, whatsoever ye shall ask in prayer, believing, ye shall receive." "All things whatsoever ye pray and ask for, believe that ye receive them, and ye shall have them." But we pray, and we pray amiss, because often we do not understand prayer.

What is prayer? It is aspiration toward God. We might say communion with God; but we are not practicing true prayer if we are telling God about all our troubles and difficulties and begging Him to do something about them. We associate "telling" with "communing." So I like the word aspiration better, because we are aspiring to be what God is. For are we not a part of Him? And are we not then aspiring toward our true self?

To mention our troubles in our prayers is to pray amiss. We want what we pray about, and we certainly do not want our troubles, our lack, our sickness. In our prayers we are to talk and think about what we desire, and not what is seemingly ours already, for seemingly we have sickness, loneliness, and unhappiness.

Emmet Fox said in *The Golden Key:* "Stop thinking about the difficulty, whatever it is, and think about God instead." It does not make any difference what kind of trouble ours is. The same rule holds. Refuse to support with your mind the thing you do not want.

Man is so constructed, in the image and likeness of God, that he has his Father's imaging power. He brings forth by imaging, and he can image that which is not good while he prays just as easily as he can image Truth or good. When we pray we should use this power of imaging and aspire toward God. Think what God is. We know He is perfection, wholeness, completeness, all good. Then let us aspire toward these things.

Perfection means being possessed of all wisdom, filled with love, forever in harmony with the good. Think then about wisdom, aspire to be wise, and claim the wisdom that comes to you from God. Claim the love of God.

Wholeness means being whole in body and soul. Think of your body as perfect and whole, regardless of what it may seem to be. Remember that the body is the fruit of the mind. Aspire toward divine wholeness. Claim that God fills every cell of your body and you are perfect and whole. Do not spend an extra moment in worrying about any part of the body wherein you seem to be ill, for that is admitting something other than perfection. Be true to your prayer. Say to every part of your body: "You are perfect and whole, and every cell is alive and alight with God."

Completeness embraces every phase of your life.

Your life is satisfying, complete, orderly. Aspire toward this. Claim it. Completeness in soul development means that we are to have all the friends and loved ones we need to attain it. If we do not have them it is because we are not thinking steadfastly of what we want, and therefore we are not drawing them to us. Perhaps we are spending too much time thinking of what we do not have, and our lack remains with us or perhaps becomes greater. Claim loving friends, give thanks for someone to cherish and love, and these will come into your outer vision and fill the seeming void.

Completeness also includes all the money and outer things that we need. These come from God too and are brought into manifestation in exactly the same way: by our aspiring toward them and associating mentally with them; not by our thinking about poverty, but by our claiming and thinking about plenty. We cannot claim the good while our mind is filled with "evil," for the law of mind action runs thus: That which man holds in mind will come forth into outer expression.

It is hard for us to let go of our troubles, but unless we desire them to be increased a hundredfold we must close them out of our mind. For the mind is like the soil, ready to bring forth fruit after the kind of seed placed in it. We are not to form a picture of God but to claim all that we know that God is; and God is wisdom, He is love, substance, supply. God is all good. God is our life.

Think on these things, claim them, and press your claims until they come into visibility. Think on those things which are lovely, real, and good; then return to principle and have faith and believe in them, not in something negative that may happen, or that seems to be happening. Know that there is but one presence in the world. Then what kind of thinking are we engaged in when we doubt that our prayer will be answered, giving power to thinking that is not of God? We are giving power to negative thoughts.

We should "take no thought," Jesus said, about anything that is unlike God, good. We are not to get discouraged if our prayer is not answered immediately. The farmer does not dig up his seed after he has planted it to see if it is growing, for if he did he knows it would never grow. But he waits upon the law, the Lord. He depends on God to do His part, and he knows the crop will bear fruit according to the seed sown.

We know that in God's world there are many inescapable truths. We know that if we sow wheat we get wheat. If we sow onions we get onions. No one would be so foolish as to think that after sowing corn he could reap oats. If it were otherwise chaos would result, for there would be no order in God's world and we could not be certain of anything. The result would be something like an experience that happened in my husband's family when he was a little boy.

He was a member of a large family, and his
father was in the habit of buying dozens of cases of
all kinds of canned vegetables and fruit, which he
stored in the attic until they were needed. One day
while my husband and one of his brothers were play-
ing in the attic they conceived the idea of unpack-
ing all of the boxes of canned goods and tearing the
labels off the cans. His mother had a nerve-racking
time that winter, for she never knew what the next
can she opened would contain.

We can hardly imagine how it would be possible
to live in a world where corresponding confusion
existed. We know that when we sow seed we shall
reap with exactness the harvest of that seed. There
is no escaping this law of God. Man's praying works
in exactly the same way as does his seed planting,
and man often is praying when he least realizes it.

Whatever we spend a great deal of time thinking
about, we are meditating on, and meditation is a
part of praying. When we spend much time thinking
about something, we are sowing it in the garden of
the mind, even though it is the last thing in the
world we should desire to have come forth in our
life. For as we sow in the garden of the mind so
shall we reap in body and affairs. Let us be sure
that we are meditating upon the good. Meditation
should be a waiting upon inspiration from God.

Prayer then is aspiration, and prayer and meditation open the way for inspiration. Both aspiration
and inspiration are important, and one is not com-

plete without the other. Prayer may be likened to the preparing of the soil and the sowing of the seed by the farmer, while meditation may be compared to a waiting upon God to fulfill His promise, a waiting upon the thought seed to come forth.

We should not beg God for our good. Did not Jesus say our heritage was prepared for us from the beginning and is ours by divine right? If we are not receiving all good we are not accepting and living up to our true heritage. To beg God for what is ours by divine right is as silly as going to the bank and getting down on our knees and begging the teller to give us our money. We would be begging for what is ours by right and for what we may obtain by claiming it, accepting it, and giving thanks for it.

We have become a world of praying beggars. Yet begging is wasted breath, because we cannot change God by begging Him for what we want. Would we have any respect for a God that could be changed by mere begging or pleading? No! We cannot change God. God, the good, is here. We must accept Him, the good, by claiming and pressing our claim until we receive. For it is really we who must take the good that God is, that we are a part of, and that came with us in the beginning. We are cut off from this good only in mind.

On many occasions we really refuse the good and claim and hold to the things we think are not good. We must accept the good. Our prayers are often not answered as we would want them to be because we can not see how God can work it out; we do not believe in our own prayers.

If we are praying certain words with our mouths and believing the opposite of them in our hearts, our prayers will not be answered. We must get our expectations and our prayers together. When we fail to do so our prayers become the kind that Jesus warned us against: vain repetitions. He did not warn us against repetition, but against *vain* repetition.

When we pray, it is well to speak the words aloud or silently, think about them, concentrate on them. Remember the words must always express the desire for completeness, never lack. Say them over quietly.

For instance, if we are praying for health, we are to claim that we are one with God according to the words of Jesus Christ. Therefore we must be all that God is, perfection and wholeness; because we cannot be a part of Him and be less than He is.

After we have said the words quietly, we should think upon them, image them, and then let go of the prayer.

It is well to pray only until a peaceful feeling comes within us. This will not take long if we think upon the good, the real, and concentrate upon it and speak of it. God is within us, and He hears us. He knows what we have need of, for is He not the desire within us that tells us what we need? Of course He is. He is nearer than hands and feet, for His connection with us is in our mind.

Even God cannot get over to us the idea that will solve all our difficulties if our mind is so full of fear and doubt that there is no place for Him in it.

When we pray we must open our mind to good. We must know that the desire within us that makes us feel the need of praying is God urging us on to the highest attainment. We must know that the desire is God, saying, "This is the thing you need, and it is yours." But we must claim it, not vainly by repeating our prayer over and over because we cannot see the way that He can bring about our good, but quietly, knowing that He can accomplish it, for God is the answer as well as the prayer. He is the desire, the fulfilling power, and the answer. God is all, and He cannot fail.

If you believe and know that He can do all things then He can. Just try it.

Most of our prayers are not answered because we shut God out. We cannot see the answer to our prayer and so we close the door on God. Or perhaps we want our prayer answered in a certain way and will accept no other. God has ways we know not of in which to perform His wonders. Let us not try to outline the way to God. Let us hold to the good we desire, the goal, whether it be happiness, peace, love, wisdom, abundance, or health, and hold to the final goal, the completed thing. Let God fill in the plan. Let Him put in the details. We do not need to know how He will do it.

Let us make contact with the divine source of good as we would tap the source of light by plugging a lamp into a socket. God will do the rest. The light will shine. He will show us step by step how to go each day if we will but let Him. Let us keep our plans and our minds out of the way. Let us turn the desire in our hearts over to God, and then resolutely refuse to take it back into our hands or our minds.

Prayer is worship, true worship. Prayer is the solvent that dissolves all our past mistakes and fears into nothingness. Let us turn from our problem and trust our bountiful Father. We do not need to know how He will answer our prayer, for God's ways are not man's ways; but we do know that by praying we supplement our finite strength with energy from the source of all energy, with the power that spins the universe. "In the heart of man a cry—in the heart of God supply."

As we ask believing, our human lacks are filled. Someone has said: "Prayer is like radium; it is a source of luminous, self-generating energy." As we pray we see ourselves. Sometimes we see our selfishness, silly pride, fear, greed, and blunders, and we become humble, like a little child. Then we are ready for the kingdom. As we pray let us not pray that God may think of us, but that we may remember God!

It was Lincoln to whom someone said, "We trust, Sir, that God is on our side." "It is more important to know that we are on God's side," Lincoln replied.

We can pray anywhere, in the street, the office, the shop, the schoolroom, in the solitude of our room, amid the crowd in a church. If we are to be one with God, prayer must become a habit. It is foolish to pray in the morning and live and think negatively all day. True prayer is a way of life, and we must live it every moment. All we need to do is turn toward God. He fills us with His love and peace. Today as never before prayer is a universal necessity in the lives of men and nations.

Prayer is the exercise of the Spirit, and it is the lack of knowledge of Spirit that has brought the world to the edge of destruction. Many of us have failed to develop this deepest source of our power and protection—prayer. Man must pray. The common man, the great man, all men must pray so that this power may be released to make a better world.

Our slightest impulse to pray is recognized by God. We do not need to say a long formal prayer. Our prayer may be wholly mental, but it must be a mental claiming of the highest. God reaches man through the quietness and silence of mind. So let us prepare the place where we are to meet Him.

FOR MEDITATION

I make prayer the first practice in my life; I have constant contact with the source of all good.
                                        —*Sue Sikking.*

The Power of Nonresistance

REMEMBER that the best conductor of electricity is the substance that is least resistant to the flow of the electric current. Likewise the best conductor of divine power is the person who is nonresistant to the flow of divine power.

Divine power is the greatest power in the universe, and it is expressed in many forms. One of the most important of these is love. The man who would receive divine love freely must not resist its inflow, nor must he resist its outflow to his fellow men.

Nonresistance means more than not resisting things and people in the physical world. It means being nonresistant as regards human thoughts and emotions. A person may refuse to fight or to speak angry words, but at the same time he may boil inwardly with resistant thoughts and emotions. Such a person is far from being nonresistant, though he knows how to hold his temper.

If a man would be nonresistant he must be nonresistant in all three departments of his being, in spirit, soul, and body. When he is nonresistant only in his bodily actions and words, while his soul seethes with anger, he is resistant to divine power and his resistance creates discord within himself, which is harmful to his health and peace of mind.

How can a man become nonresistant? By following the spirit of the teachings of Jesus Christ any man can discipline his personal ego and make it less resistant to the power of God working through him. Jesus Christ was so nonresistant that God was able to do His mighty works through Him. Jesus Christ multiplied the loaves and fishes, cast out demons, healed the lepers, and raised the dead; and He promised that those who followed Him would be able to do even greater things. Read the Sermon on the Mount and you will see that many of its teachings aim at the disciplining of the human ego so that it may become more nonresistant.

The secret of becoming nonresistant is to bring the personal ego under the control of the I AM. When this is done the Christ will have greater freedom of expression in the individual man.

It is the nature of the personal ego to be proud and to dote on the possession of worldly power and riches, but Jesus taught, "The meek . . . shall inherit the earth." The personal ego would humble or destroy an adversary by physical force or argument, but Jesus taught, "Agree with thine adversary quickly."

It is possible for even a church member to act in an unchristian way at times when influenced by his personal ego, even though he aspires to do good and be righteous. Before his ego is thoroughly disciplined a would-be follower of Christ is prone to fight those who do evil, but Jesus said: "Resist not him that is evil." "And whosoever shall compel thee to go one mile, go with him two. . . . Love your enemies, and pray for them that persecute you."

These precepts may seem negative and impractical to the so-called practical man of the world, when his personal ego urges him to take what he wants by force if need be. But after all, this is the hard way to success. The method of gaining things by force fails to bring real joy and satisfaction into the life of the one who depends upon it.

Consider some of the great military conquerors of the past, Julius Caesar, for instance, and more recently Hitler. Their victories brought them little soul satisfaction or enduring power.

On the other hand, Jesus Christ has more followers and power today than He had when He was on earth. This shows that the kind of power He exercised was different from the worldly kind for which men strive. Jesus was nonresistant to the point where He was able to forgive even those who were crucifying Him. Perfectly nonresistant to the will of God, He opened the way for God's power to come into His body and soul with such a surge that He was resurrected on the third day after He was put in the tomb.

Divine power enabled Jesus to overcome the world, the flesh, and the Devil, and He expects His disciples—those who are under spiritual discipline— to win victories over all the difficulties that beset them in the world by using the tremendous power of nonresistance.

God's will for all His children is that they may

be healthy, prosperous, and happy here and now in the world. Those who co-operate with Him in bringing His kingdom into the world do gain these things. Those who fight and strive selfishly for power, place, and possessions must be aware that something is wrong with their methods, because they experience so much strife in dealing with their fellow men. They cannot feel the inner satisfaction that God is more willing to give than they are to receive.

It does not require great material riches and power to satisfy man's inner hunger, for the power of God working freely through him can supply all that he needs. God knows what we need before we ask, and His supply is boundless.

What merely rich and powerful man can feed five thousand persons with a few loaves and fishes? What great military man, who is able to kill thousands, can resurrect even one dead person? The man of the world can destroy plants, trees, and animals, but he cannot create these things.

There is a quiet power in nature that is constantly renewing the forests and the growing fields destroyed by man. Man cannot truly destroy life nor can he create it. The life principle is eternal, and when a man becomes sufficiently nonresistant he masters death, the last enemy.

A man may not at once attain all the blessings that God has intended he should enjoy, but with every step he takes toward self-control and nonresistance he gains additional riches of the kingdom now at this time.

The kingdom of heaven is at hand, but only the nonresistant man can receive it. Here it is true that the first shall be last and the last shall be first. To the worldly observer the last often seems to be last because he is not aggressive; actually he is first because he is nonresistant. The power of God lifts the meek man and sets him on high because he is willing to be lifted. That a person seems timid and backward is no sign that he is truly nonresistant. He may be stubborn and selfish at heart but afraid to fight. A person who is absolutely nonresistant toward God has no fear of anybody or anything. His faith in the power of God makes him fearless to do what is right, knowing that in doing right he is backed up by the greatest power in the universe.

No worry, doubt, fear, jealousy, greed, or lust can exist in one who is nonresistant toward God. The nonresister is able to receive everything he needs to sustain life, and he need not worry about anything or fear anybody. Nothing that matters can be taken away from him.

The truly nonresistant man stands like the Rock of Gibraltar, unmoved in the sea of human discord, but unlike a rock he blossoms like the rose as his inner riches, the fruits of Spirit are made manifest.

Do not be afraid to put your little personal self aside to make room for your Christ self. Do not be afraid of what people will say or think about you.

You and God are a majority. Blessed are you when others persecute you if you are nonresistant enough to the will of God to stand with Christ, to whom every knee must eventually bow. You are secure when you abide in Christ.

FOR MEDITATION

I do not resist evil; I make myself receptive only to the good.

—*Lowell Fillmore.*

Vanity

IT is curious how plainly vanity of any kind shows itself; it is as easy to see as dirt on the face. The girl who looks in the mirror at every chance; the boy who is forever combing his hair; the woman who parades before every show window; the man who indulges in pompous advertising of self—all advertise their weakness in many a way that they would avoid like a trap if they realized what they were doing.

Vanity is a trap, one of the worst traps into which we can fall, because it trips us and deceives us and blinds us disastrously. You have heard it said that "a penny held close to the eye will shut out the sun." Well, vanity is a blindfold that will shut out everything worth seeing, from lovely scenery to lovable people, from knowledge to wisdom, from beauty to God. Vanity is exclusive concern with self, and any considerable concern with self is always exclusive. It excludes so many of the best things in life that it sometimes starves people's minds and hearts.

"Be yourself" is a current phase frequently aimed at those who cultivate a pose. It is good advice; but the only way I can be my true self is to forget myself. The pretty girl who forgets herself becomes a thing of heartwinning loveliness; the smart boy who forgets himself becomes the successful man; the experienced woman who forgets herself becomes the influential leader; the able man who forgets himself becomes a power or, let us say, a channel for power.

Simple forgetfulness of self multiplies personality, makes homeliness itself beautiful, expands usefulness, makes life more abundant. I like a phrase I once read as a suggestion for becoming a good conversationalist: "Anything about yourself is too much." The only justification for talking about oneself is relating experience that is enlightening and then only when the experience and not the self gets the emphasis. When Jesus talked about Himself, it was always to emphasize His relationship to the Father as an experience that everyone could have for the asking.

But the worst feature of vanity is that it is a confining, handicapping, crippling harness. It robs one of the ability to perform almost any graceful service, from public speaking to private charity. It hinders action like hobbles on a horse or manacles on a man. It throttles ability. It saps vitality.

Self-forgetfulness, on the contrary, releases your powers. Nothing significant or of worth or consequence is ever accomplished by the self-conscious man. Nursing an overweening regard for self, for one's appearance, for one's "effect," is like putting on an antiquated suit of armor. When a man becomes so absorbed in his work or his art or his cause that he forgets himself, he is always surprised—and so are his friends—by his sudden effectiveness. A human being is like a plant that flowers and bears fruit when it has free access to rain and sun and air and room to grow. Vanity, self-concern, is as stifling as a gunny sack. A vain man is like a prisoner shut away from life.

It is self-forgetfulness that makes heroes. It is self-forgetfulness that builds health. It is self-forgetfulness that taps inspiration. It is self-forgetfulness that wins success. It is self-forgetfulness that insures usefulness.

If we could just realize that when we give up vanity we are not giving up anything of value but something tragically worthless, we would not waste much time cultivating it. But the only way to stop cultivating it is to ignore self-interest. If we seek credit for performance, we are most likely to lose it. If we seek preferment, we are disappointed more often than not. If we fish for compliments, we catch shame. If we strut, we stumble. If we try to stand alone, we fall.

Paul said that "Love . . . seeketh not its own." He admonished the brethren to be affectionate, "in honor preferring one another." The Master's life is a perfect example of self-forgetfulness. We marvel at the power that was released in Him.

If you want to write or paint or invent or perform, you have to rid yourself of constant concern with praise and applause. Greatness will not be had except at the price of humility. Fun cannot be created by vanity, except by ridiculing it. The greatest greatness is born when all thought of self is lost. The funniest fun is actually making fun of oneself.

Vanity is a weakness that perfectly illustrates our curious tendency to grasp for what seems immediate profit without regard for the ultimate gain. Maybe it will help us to remember the soap bubble when we are tempted to be "puffed up," which is another thing Paul says love does not permit.

Now what is the technique for getting rid of vanity, self-concern? We cannot get rid of it by trying to get rid of it. We might as well try to change our eyes from brown to blue. There is only one way to forget self and that is to love others. "Well," some discouraged one mourns, "how can I love others when I don't?"

There are two ways, closely allied. One way to love another is deliberately to study to understand him, his circumstances, his environment, his education, his endowments, his situation in life; and to realize that he is cast in the same mold we are, with the same hopes and fears, ambitions and aspirations, desires and weaknesses, struggles and loves. "When all is understood, all is forgiven." When we understand a man thoroughly we shall begin to feel kindly toward him, perhaps in pity at first, which is proverbially akin to love.

The second way to learn to love another is to begin doing something for him, something genuinely beneficial and helpful, without seeking credit for it, which spoils it. Do it for him unselfishly, generously, self-forgetfully. That is the truest expression of love, and it is the best seed from which love grows. Do unselfish things for anybody and you will come to love him. That is the secret of the marvelous devotion to causes that we find it so hard to understand until we give some service ourselves.

Of course by the same token this is the way to learn to love God. Begin to serve Him and you cannot help loving Him. Sometimes we tell ourselves that it is because of what He gives us that we love Him. But it is far more because of what we give Him.

You cannot call it sacrifice; it is never sacrifice to give up some lesser thing for a greater. How terribly vanity blinds us when the essential self-love of it prevents our learning to love God!

If I find myself filled with fear, something is wrong with me. Nothing can fill one with fear more surely than being blind, and there is no blindness like vanity or self-centered living. It hides the beauty of things, the loveliness of other persons, the love of God. Perfect love casteth out fear by casting out self-love.

FOR MEDITATION

I put aside thoughts of self and all petty desires; I express the Christ within me.

—Gardner Hunting.

True Security

OURS HAS been termed "the era of anxiety." Certainly we are witnessing an unprecedented search for security in today's troubled world. This is testified to by the large sale and huge popularity of "peace of mind" and "peace of soul" books. It is reflected in the wide-scale social-security programs of the various national governments, in individual planning for retirement funds, and in the increased demands for bigger pensions made on large corporations by workers.

In the field of child-training we are seeing a strong emphasis placed on the need of the infant for emotional security. We are told that he derives this security if his infantile needs for love and affection and attention are generously satisfied, so that he feels from the beginning that he is in a friendly world where people care for him and are not indifferent to his presence and his feelings. Having met friendliness, love, and co-operation from those who care for him, he is better able to get the "feel" of them and to express friendliness, love, and co-operation in his turn toward others.

These new trends in our modern world are evidences of a spiritual unfoldment that is now taking place. They show an increased recognition of the human being's need for a deep and abiding faith in the goodness of the universe—its strength, sta-

bility, and well-meaningness toward the individual.
They presage increasingly greater progress for man
in the spiritual, mental, and physical realms.

We are witnessing a demonstration on a grand
scale of the truth that whenever man recognizes a
desire in his heart, he is bound to search for its fulfillment, and when he searches, he will surely find.

It did not occur to primordial man that he was
entitled to security. He took insecurity for granted
as the order of the universe. As a cave-dweller he
saw danger lurking all about him in wind, storm, and
savage beast. Even his gods were indifferent or hostile beings who had to be placated and appeased.
The most he could hope for from them was that they
would not notice him, and let him alone. He had
no expectation that they would love him and help
him.

Even the one God of the Old Testament, in the
early days of the Hebrew race, was felt to be a
pretty sadistic one who "plagued" the people and
was forever visiting His wrath upon them. Our
pioneer ancestors in America expected no "security"
in their grim fight for survival against hostile elements and savage enemies. The wrathful God of
Jonathan Edwards' sermons reflects their expectations from the universe of trial and tribulation, and
their uncertainty of good.

So the present quest for security is a good and
salutary sign. Even in the face of the three atomic
warfare, man begins to believe in his good. Some-

thing deep in his heart cries out for it and senses his kinship with it. His restless search for it shows that he begins to realize that as a human being and a son of God he is entitled to it. And what he expands his consciousness to recognize and claim for himself, he will achieve.

But in looking to outer means to provide the security that man inwardly knows belongs to him, he is not looking far enough. These outer means are good as far as they go, but man needs to discern and place his faith in the true source of security.

The truth is that man's only real security lies in God and in the divinity within himself that makes him one with God. Man must look within, not without, for the peace of heart and soul he craves and now senses is his inborn right. Not in pensions, annuities, insurance policies, government agencies, labor unions, or man-made laws lies his true security, although these are agencies through which it operates in part.

Even the emphasis in modern child-training on parental love in assuring a child's emotional security is only a fragmentary portion of the whole. It is a foreshadowing of the real, a symbol of the actual, a prototype of the true security that is man's birthright as a son of the Most High.

It is from and through the parent that a child gets his first concept of God, and in this sense an early conditioning toward love in family relations predisposes the child toward making a happy trans-

ference to God as the source of his more lasting
security. It is for this reason, I dare say, that He
"setteth the solitary in families." Having known
and experienced a loving mother and father, the
child can the more easily and naturally believe in a
loving God who cares for him.

A small boy seemed quite undisturbed aboard
a great ship that pitched and tossed in enormous
waves during a storm at sea. All the other pas-
sengers were terrified. One of them asked him,
"Aren't you afraid?" The child laughed and said
serenely, "Afraid? Oh, no, I'm not afraid. My father is the captain."

When we have men and women whose childhood
faith in a good parent is merged gradually into faith
in God and the essential goodness and worthiness
of all His other children on this planet, then we
have men and women who are ready to claim and
enjoy their true security in life. It is the only kind
of security that lasts, for about it there is a permanence that justifies the real derivation of the word's
meaning. It comes from two small Latin ones, *se,*
without, and *cura,* care. Without care! Free from
fear or anxiety. Easy in mind. Safe. Think of it!
Not for a little time either. Not just this month or
next year or ten years from now, but forever.

The security that men are grasping for in terms
of material things is unstable, because it is based
upon shifting standards of value. A "safe" invest-
ment does not always remain "safe," and an old-age

retirement plan may prove to be inadequate in the face of high prices. Parents and loved ones may go out of our life. If our plan is to derive a sense of security from our own achievements, we are likely to feel disappointed and frustrated if advancing age hinders us from keeping to a high standard of performance in our trade or profession.

In short, when we place our security in the temporal and material, be it money, possessions, accomplishments, friends, loved ones, we are likely to meet disappointment and disillusionment and find ourselves lost when we most need to feel secure and safe. In the words of the old hymn, "Change and decay in all around I see." But the hymn does not leave us there, does it? It goes on with that glorious cry, "Oh, Thou who changest not, abide with me." And somehow we sense that this is not a child's cry in the dark, or a desperate plea for help, but a calm assumption of assurance. He "who failest not" cannot fail us either, cannot possibly fail to abide with us if we will have it that way.

In the Bible the now popular term "security" is used infrequently and then in the sense that our banks use it when they require security against a loan. But that does not mean that you will not find in the Bible plenty of the sort of security we are talking about. It is the "peace of mind" and "peace of soul" book without parallel in the world. The word "peace" is used over two hundred times in its pages, and "confidence" in its various forms about

fifty times. Thus we have such great comforting
assurances as "faith is of things hoped for a confidence." "In quietness and in confidence shall be
your strength."

"For Jehovah shall be thy confidence,
    And will keep thy foot from being taken."

The Bible is a treasure-trove of security for you,
no matter what your need. Open it at almost any
page and lay hold on that security. Here are a few
samples of the kind you will find there:

"Let not your heart be troubled; believe in God,
believe also in me." (What bond in your safety
deposit vault can say that to you?)

"Underneath are the everlasting arms." (What
else is everlasting that you have tried to depend
on?)

"When thou liest down, thou shalt not be afraid:
  Yea, thou shalt lie down, and thy sleep shall be
        sweet."

  "For he will give his angels charge over thee,
    To keep thee in all thy ways."

(Still afraid of atom bombs? Read the whole of
the 91st Psalm and you will not be. It is the security
Psalms par excellence and never fails to cure you of
the jitters or false alarms.)

I talked about some of these things to a troubled
adolescent recently. He said, "How do you know
you aren't just kidding yourself about all this?
Maybe it's wishful thinking. After all, you can't
prove it. Nobody's ever *seen* God. How do you know

you're not inventing Him? How do you know you aren't looking for crutches?"

This is an old question that crops up often from the factual-minded young who test compounds in school laboratories and move among test tubes and breakers and Bunsen burners. They want to weigh, measure, and analyze. We must think through the question when they raise it and be prepared to answer it honestly and without an impatience that alienates them or makes them feel that we are not too sure of our ground. This is substantially what I told him:

"If you are going to be a doubter, you must at least be an honest one and fair enough to doubt your doubts too. It says in the Bible, 'No man hath seen God at any time.' But neither has any man ever seen some things that our hearts tell us are true.

"We have never seen love but we live by it and experience it richly every day. We have never seen joy but the times when we feel it are our happy moments, too, when we feel closest to our destiny and our reason for being alive at all. We have never seen life but it animates our bodies, which are not in themselves life but only an expression of it. We do not see life born and we do not see it die. We only see bodies born and bodies die. We do not see life leave a body when it dies but we know that something is gone which a moment before was there, something real, and powerful, and vital, yet unseen.

"We do not see the inspiration we get from a fine symphony concert but it stirs and animates us. To move us so deeply it must be real; something does not come from nothing. We do not see courage, or sympathy, or fortitude, or faith, but they motivate us and because of them we accomplish great things in the world that would not otherwise get done or be here in our world as a testimony to the Unseen. We do not even see the air we breathe. But if you want to deny it exists, simply hold your breath long enough and you will very shortly know why it is always a good idea to doubt your doubts!"

In believing in God as our true security, we are not depending on crutches. We are throwing our crutches away. Crutches are the supports we depend on in the temporal, material world—enough money, fine possessions, a superior education, pride in profession or achievement, friends, loved ones, special privileges. Some of these things are fine. But they are not our true security because they cannot possibly last forever and there is not one among them that is infallible. You cannot see God, but paradoxically you can find Him very easily. For, as the Bible says, "No man hath beheld God at any time: if we love one another, God abideth in us, and his love is perfected in us: hereby we know that we abide in him and he in us, because he hath given us of his Spirit. . . . God is love; and he that abideth in love abideth in God, and God abideth in him."

To know this is to find the only real security life has to offer us, the dynamic security that comes from within, derived from orienting ourselves toward the infinite, the unchanging, the everlasting. These are the "Before Abraham was born, I am" values. Any other kind of security is not security at all. For it is man-made, not God-made security.

FOR MEDITATION

God is my eternal resource, my unfailing security.

—Constance J. Foster.

Praise

PRAISE IS A FORM of prayer that recognizes Spirit back of every desire or need. Praise is a form of blessing, a way of life. When you feel an urge to criticize, to hate, to find fault, to get angry and use bitter words, creating chaos in yourself and your environment, stop for a moment and realize that kindness, love, and praise are mighty forces for good in your life and in the lives of those about you. If instead of condemning we would praise the good in all things and in all people we should find that praise, like love, "never faileth." Praising the Christ in ourselves awakens us to see the Christ in others. No unhappiness or discord can enter our world when it is full to overflowing with praise.

One of the surest ways to bring good into manifestation is to praise it, give thanks for it, and bless it even before it is manifest. We should be as lavish in our praise of all good, both manifest and unmanifest, as God is lavish in bestowing His blessings and love upon us.

"Praise the name of Jehovah your God, that hath dealt wondrously with you."

Praise and bless the goodness of God in all men and in all things. Regardless of outer appearances, we can always be sure of the inner presence of God's goodness. Praising and magnifying the good calls that good forth into fuller expression.

Praise is a channel through which the most bountiful blessings of God flow to us. Praise attracts good to us because through it we draw close to God. Praise helps us to develop joy, love, harmony, and all the positive qualities and elements that draw our good to us. Praise gives us a feeling of oneness with God. It lifts us up into the consciousness of our sonship with Him. The more we praise the easier it becomes, until we form a habit of praise, making it easy for us to see and express the good of God to all about us.

Praise is a great solvent, a powerful harmonizing force that we can use in every walk of life. Praise is not flattery, it is not blarney. Praise is kindness, giving honor where honor is due, acknowledging the good wherever found.

There is no better way to help ourselves than to behold the Christ in others. There is no higher form of praise than this. It pays to take time to understand ourselves and our fellow men. If we find it difficult to forgive others for their seeming short comings let us look beyond the human frailty and praise the Christ within. Every experience that comes into our life holds some lesson for good if we will look for it. Praise is a great liberating power; there is nothing more effective for enlivening the soul and quickening the Spirit.

If you desire better health or more life, praise and give thanks for your perfect life and health in God. Praise God until you feel every cell and nerve and atom of your being vibrating with new life.

Praise and give thanks that abundance and joy are now being manifested in your life and in all your affairs.

As we praise and give thanks to God for the blessings in our life we raise our consciousness to the realization that we are receiving richly and bountifully all that the Father has to give. As we praise and give thanks for the seeming small blessings that go to make up our life and the lives of those about us we put into action the law of increase and our blessings grow, our life becomes rich and full and joyous. We live gloriously; we keep in mind that we are sons of God; we see all good as God come forth into manifestation. For His eternal, ever-present good we continually praise His holy name.

Praise causes good to spring into manifestation. We praise the health that we have and see it increase. We praise the money that we have and see it multiply. We praise our affairs and see them divinely adjusted. If we praise even the smallest bit of good that comes to us we shall soon find good springing up on every hand. Praise makes us radiant and optimistic. Praise from one we respect or love fills us with joy and gladness. When we praise anything we set into operation a force that has magical multiplying and increasing power.

There are many persons about us who are in need of praise. They need to be sustained by loving words in time of discouragement. Our word of praise serves to give them a higher vision of themselves, of their worth to God, and of their worth to humanity. Quite often a word of praise from us is sufficient to inspire another to do his best work. A word of praise from us may steady another at a time of wavering or encourage him in a moment of doubt and despair. To praise another causes him to rise to the best of which he is capable. He is inspired to perceive himself as he is in Christ.

When we condemn another or ourselves we lower our spiritual vision. Instead of taking ourselves to task for something we have said or done we should seek to measure ourselves by the standard of our Christ perfection. Instead of criticising we should praise. Instead of looking at our shortcomings we should try to see perfection in all that we do. "This is the way, walk ye in it."

Praise has magic in it. It will cause our blessings to multiply and increase. It will help us to discover blessings that we did not know existed. Look about you today for something or someone to praise. Cease to pronounce adverse judgment on other persons. Stop criticising and condemning and start praising. Blessings are everywhere around us. They are ours to enjoy. They are gifts from God to us. If we feel that we do not have any blessings in life let us get quiet and look for at least one thing for which we can be thankful, for one thing that we can honestly praise in ourselves, our affairs, or our environment. This knowledge will give us a new slant on life.

The word of praise when set in operation in our financial affairs causes our prosperity to increase. Praise your business and you will soon discover that others have taken up the idea of praising it. Your word of praise causes your good to appear. You cannot believe in poverty when your consciousness is filled with thoughts of prosperity and praise.

Turn the battery of praise upon whatever you wish to increase. Praise every evidence of the goodness of God. Give thanks for what you have and you will find that you have more for which to be thankful. The appreciative person naturally draws many blessings to himself. Our ability to be grateful and thankful for what we receive causes us to receive richly. Praising our good will cause it to increase and prosper. Applying the law of praise to our affairs will prove to us the working of the law.

We should make seeing the good a habit of our life. Every moment of the day, no matter where we are or what we are doing, God, the good, is within us and about us. Praise His holy name in all creation.

Praise should be used with reference to conditions and things as well as persons. The habit of praise should be cultivated. We cannot be reminded too often of the stupendous power for good that lies in praise. We should give immediate expression to all the praise we feel, for by so doing we magnify and increase the good for which we are grateful and at the same time we prepare ourselves to receive and to use more good.

Many times we take the wrong attitude toward things. Back of every negative experience that comes to us is a lack of understanding. The lack of understanding may be the result of a wrong viewpoint or of a failure to see past outer appearances and to discern the spiritual idea back of the experience in question. Sometimes the apparent adversary is in the form of a condition or circumstance. It is obvious that the admonition to agree with our adversary is designed to tell us to get an understanding of the person or condition to be met. When it becomes necessary to agree with an adversary we should try to find something about him to praise. Praise costs nothing, but it gives much. It enriches both the one who gives and the one who receives. Praise creates happiness in the home, fosters good will in business, is a countersign of friendship. It brings new hope and cheer to the discouraged, sunshine to the sad. It is one of the world's best antidotes for trouble.

A good word that is sincerely spoken blesses the one who speaks it as well as the one to whom it is spoken. Perfect harmony with God's children is an indication of perfect harmony with God. There are people around us all who are literally starving for a word of praise. If we know such a person, right now is the time for us to prove the power of praise. Every day we can declare the Truth for him. Every day we can silently bless the good in him. Honest praise is far better than the most kindly meant criticism. A bit of praise will soothe and relax taut nerves and bring them into perfect harmony with God's great symphony of life.

How can we praise and approve of a condition that manifestly is not good? We can praise it for the opportunity it gives us to find and use a power greater than the evil of imperfection that the condition represents to us. We shall make our agreement not with the evil that appears but with the good that we expect to appear through the power of our praise.

Praise has been called the great liberator. In the story of Paul and Silas they are said to have lain in jail bound with chains, but instead of giving up to despair they rejoiced and sang hymns of praise and the very walls of the prison were shaken down, setting them free. We too can sing songs of praise when the cares of our world seem to bind us and fill us with despair. We can praise the never-failing Presence in us and about us until our shackles are loosed and the walls of our doubt and fear are shaken down.

A word of praise will raise the spirits of one involved in difficulties and produce a sense of elation in the soul of the praiser. Few of us realize the full potency of praise. Appreciation and praise of what we have will free us from greed and longing and unrest for things not instantly available. To praise whatever good we can see and to praise silently what we know of God's goodness will even develop good out of seeming lack and limitation, although it may be invisible at the present moment.

Praise is a master key of life. Have you ever noticed how praise makes the eyes shine and the face light up; how it lightens labor and brightens the shop and home environment? Have you ever stood before a mirror when you felt dejected and blue and consciously looked for something to praise about yourself? And have you seen your countenance light up and your depression vanish at the happy thought?

If we want more appreciation ourselves we must be more appreciative of others. Just as we must first give more love if we want more love in our own life, so we must first make sure that we are giving more praise if we want more praise for ourselves. Begin now to praise, silently if need be, the members of your own family, your business associates, your seeming enemies. Begin to look for and find good in everybody and everything in your entire world.

Praise, like love, is a mighty power within us. Love and praise make others happy as well as ourselves. Praise is like inner sunshine; it warms the heart of the giver as well as the heart of the receiver. Praise enriches the lives of all who receive it. Try praising something about someone you think you do not like. Then watch him respond to your kind words sincerely given. You will make more friends in a week by sincere praise honestly given than you will make in a year by criticism no matter how truthful it may seem to you.

Friendliness is the twin brother to praise. Friendliness draws people of all races and creeds together.

Friendliness will give you self-satisfaction, influence in your community, a power with people that all the money in the world cannot buy. Friendliness is silent praise of another's worth. Don't wait to see if people are going to like you. Like them first. Don't wait for another to greet you. Greet him first. Give him the first smile. Give him a cheery greeting. It is silent praise of his worth, his importance to you. Everyone you meet will love you for your cheerfulness, your friendliness, your silent praise. And doesn't it make you feel good, doesn't it raise your morale to know that your bit of praise has given someone a needed lift, a thrill of pleasure, calmed and smoothed the troubled waters?

Praise is caring, caring for one of God's children, caring as Jesus cared, caring enough to say the kind word, the helpful word, the needed word. Praise calls out all that is best in us and directs it to the purpose we have before us. Praise harmonizes our whole nature and works such miracles that it literally transforms people and things. Praise bestows new life, calls latent talents into activity, lifts one from the drudgery of living into the freedom of manifestation of divine perfection. Praise lifts us out of the consciousness of mundane affairs into that of higher vision of dreams materialized. Bodies are healed, lagging business is stepped up, near failure becomes success through the power of praise.

To withhold criticism is not enough, we must recognize latent ability and praise it into life. Praise and magnify the good wherever you find it. Praise your work. Praise all the tasks that fall to your lot to do. Praise the life that is in you. Praise the life that is in your neighbor.

"Let everything that hath breath praise Jehovah."

FOR MEDITATION

I praise and bless the goodness of God in all men and in all things, and my good is magnified.
—*L. Stevens Hatfield.*

Publishers' Announcement

A More Wonderful You is published by the Unity School of Christianity, an independent educational institution devoted to teaching the principles of Christianity and the application of these principles to everyday life and affairs. In addition to *A More Wonderful You* Unity School publishes the following other books:

ATOM-SMASHING POWER OF MIND, *by Charles Fillmore*
BE! *by James Dillet Freeman*
BE OF GOOD COURAGE, *by Frank B. Whitney*
BEGINNING AGAIN, *by Frank B. Whitney*
BEST-LOVED UNITY POEMS, *an anthology*
BOTH RICHES AND HONOR, *by Annie Rix Militz*
CHRIST ENTHRONED IN MAN, *by Cora Fillmore*
CHRISTIAN HEALING, *by Charles Fillmore*
DIVINE REMEDIES, *a compilation*
DOCTOR HOUSTON SPEAKING, *by Zelia M. Walters*
EFFECTUAL PRAYER, *by Frances W. Foulks*
FAVORITE UNITY RADIO TALKS, *a collection*
GOD A PRESENT HELP, *by H. Emilie Cady*
GOD NEVER FAILS, *by Mary L. Kupferle*
GOD IS THE ANSWER, *by Dana Gatlin*
GREAT PHYSICIAN, THE, *by Ernest C. Wilson*
HAVE WE LIVED BEFORE, *by Ernest C. Wilson*
HOW I USED TRUTH, *by H. Emilie Cady*
HOW TO LET GOD HELP YOU, *by Myrtle Fillmore*
JESUS CHRIST HEALS, *by Charles Fillmore*
KEEP A TRUE LENT, *by Charles Fillmore*
KNOW THYSELF, *by Richard Lynch*
LESSONS IN TRUTH, *by H. Emilie Cady*
LET THERE BE LIGHT, *by Elizabeth Sand Turner* ($3)
LOVINGLY IN THE HANDS OF THE FATHER, *by Evelyn Whitell*
MIGHTIER THAN CIRCUMSTANCE, *by Frank B. Whitney*
MYRTLE FILLMORE'S HEALING LETTERS, *a collection*
MYSTERIES OF GENESIS, *by Charles Fillmore* ($3)

These books cover so many subjects of general and vital interest that among them you are sure to find one that meets a need of your own or that of a friend. Beautifully bound, these lovely Unity books are priced at $2 each, unless otherwise indicated.

UNITY SCHOOL OF CHRISTIANITY
Lee's Summit, Missouri

PRINTED U.S.A   6F-7500-2-59